Shri
Narasimha
Swami
Apostle of Shirdi Sai Baba

Born: 21 August, 1874   Mahasamadhi: 19 October, 1956

"I searched for a 'Sadguru' all over - in the South, in the East and, in the West. When I came to Shirdi, I found Him in my heart."

"I wandered ceaselessly. I went to many places and met many great beings. Still I wandered on. My spiritual hunger was not satisfied till I came over to Shirdi and saw Sai Baba face to face. He stopped my wandering – and with this the wandering of many. At Shirdi, I was given more than I could take. I had at last discovered my 'Sadguru'. He is Sainatha Sad-

Shri
Narasimha
Swami
Apostle of Shirdi Sai Baba

Dr G.R. Vijayakumar

Sterling Paperbacks

STERLING PAPERBACKS
An imprint of
Sterling Publishers (P) Ltd.
A-59, Okhla Industrial Area, Phase-II,
New Delhi-110020.
Tel: 26387070, 26386209; Fax: 91-11-26383788
E-mail: sterlingpublishers@airtelmail.in
ghai@nde.vsnl.net.in
www.sterlingpublishers.com

Sri Narasimha Swami: Apostle of Shirdi Sai Baba
© 2009, Sterling Publishers Pvt. Ltd.
ISBN 978- 81-207-9454-2

The book was earlier published under the title
As the Flower Sheds its Fragrance
by Sri Sai Spiritual Centre
Thyagarajanagar, Bangalore 560028

Cover drawing by Mohit Suneja

Printed and Published by Sterling Publishers Pvt. Ltd.,
New Delhi-110 020.

Dedication

This humble offering is placed
at the holy feet of
Sadguru Sri Narasimha Swamiji
whose inspired zeal and matchless dedication
discovered and presented to the troubled world
Sai Baba, the Saviour par excellence.

Our obeisance to Gurudev,
Sadguru Sri Radhakrishna Swamiji
who is always close upon our thoughts and
looking after our welfare.

Introductory Note

— ◆ —

We have pleasure in presenting this book *Sri Narasimha Swami: Apostle of Shirdi Sai Baba* – a comprehensive biography of our Parama Guru, Sri Narasimha Swamiji. In these pages, Swamiji's life has been depicted in a chronological order and the spread of Sai movement all over the country by the tireless efforts of Sri Narasimha Swamiji and his other devoted followers.

Difficult as the task was, it was a happy idea of Dr.G.R.Vijayakumar to write this biography of Sri Narasimha Swamiji and to publish it in the 50th year of Swamiji's 'Aradhana'. Dr.Vijayakumar has collected and sifted information from devotees who were closely associated with Swamiji. He has pieced together a coherent and vivid narrative.

We are grateful to our President, Sri R.Seshadri who is closely connected with the Sai movement for over five decades, for having gone through the typescript meticulously and penning a scholarly foreword.

Let me here record our sincere gratitude to Sai Baba, Sri Narasimha Swamiji and Sri Radhakrishna Swamiji for raining down their mercy upon us in the form of this spiritual biography, full of noble ideas and sentiments. Written in a charming and lucid style, this book will certainly help to engender faith in spiritual truths and encourage Sai devotees to lead a spiritual life. No doubt, this book will prove an ornament to Sai literature.

This book is an inspiring saga of the life and mission of Sri Narasimha Swamiji, which the readers will find interesting and enlightening.

Bangalore   **M.S. Jothi Raghavan**
15th March 2007   Hon. Secretary
                                                   Sri Sai Spiritual Centre

Foreword

————

Religion has been called the opiate of the people, an anachronism, an irrelevance and even a drag on progress in the modern world. This indictment is not entirely fanciful. The unfortunate emphasis on polemics and proselytisation common in organised religion has tended to obscure its true function of serving as a link between man and his Master. It was this function which the founders of the great religions exercised; it is still the driving force of the true 'seeker' today, who, in the words of Mahatma Gandhi, wants 'to strive and pine for Self-realization, to see God face to face, to attain salvation.'

It is this eternal quest, which took Sri Narasimha Swamiji to go in search for a Sadguru. He ultimately discovered for us, Sai Baba of Shirdi. Narasimha Swamiji got a big treasure of Sai grace and he distributed freely to all. In fact, Sai Baba was only confined to the remote village of Shirdi in Maharashtra prior to 1936 and it was Sri Narasimha Swamiji's untiring efforts for two decades that made Sai Baba a household name all over India.

Narasimha Swamiji met people from all walks of life and from all parts of India and indeed of the world. They include poets and artists, doctors and lawyers, scholars and civil servants, sailors and soldiers, judges, business magnates, factory workers, artisans and unlettered peasants. Among them are the shining faces of young men and women who have just left the University, and grey-haired men and women who had been searching for an anchorage all their lives. Narasimha Swamiji gave them a healing and inspiring touch. He offered them the magical formula of Sai Baba. The new life he gave to their lives through the grace of Sai Baba, is a new page in 'Bhakti Marg'.

Many have written much on Sai Baba and his Mission but hardly anything on Sri Narasimha Swamiji, whose untiring efforts made us know Sai Maharaj. This is not surprising. Saints like Narasimha Swamiji do not live in the past; he rarely kept a personal diary or wrote memoirs; and his individual self, having long since been merged in Sainath Maharaj, he had little inclination to reminisce about himself or about the past. Moreover, a spiritual odyssey is not easy to reconstruct on paper. The usual materials, the plethora of which is often the despair of the biographer and the historian, simply do not exist. There are no archives of official and non-official papers, no back volumes of newspapers and periodicals, tapes and films from which significant facts are to be gleaned. The struggles of the spirit are not waged in public view; nor are they recorded in dispatches of press correspondents; the ordeals, the travails and the triumphs of spiritual discipline have their dramatic moments, but the world knows little about them.

Difficult as the task was, it was a happy idea of Dr.G.R.Vijayakumar to write a biography of Narasimha Swamiji and to publish it on the fiftieth year of his 'Aradhana'. The printing expenses of the biography originally written in Kannada were borne by the volunteers of Sri Sai Spiritual Centre and the book was distributed to Sai devotees free of cost. This popular measure was widely appreciated and there have been persistent requests for an English version as it was felt that Swamiji's biography should reach a wider circle of readers all over the country.

Dr.Vijayakumar, a Doctor of Medicine, has been a Sai devotee since 1977 and is deeply versed in religion and philosophy. A good number of his articles have been published in several Sai magazines all over the country. He has collected and sifted information from many close associates of Narasimha Swamiji and from reminiscences of older devotees; he has pieced together a coherent and vivid narrative to make this biography really comprehensive.

Dr. Vijayakumar gives a word picture of the young Narasimha, the lively, and energetic and studious child brought up in a deeply religious and generous atmosphere. Influence of two great saints – Jagadguru Sankaracharya of Sringeri, Sri Narasimha Bharathi Swamigal and Sorakkai Swamiji in his younger days, evolution of young Narasimha Iyer into a leading lawyer, politician and a person of social eminence. A tragedy in the family acting as a turning point for his leaving the warmth and security of his home. This was a quest, which was to last more than eleven years. In his quest for God he submitted cheerfully to the most rigorous discipline of the ashrams, which sheltered him, and did not disdain the lowliest and the hardest manual labour. He travelled a great deal, mostly on foot, to different parts of the country, braving fatigue, cold and hunger. It was a self-imposed ordeal in which hope alternated with despair. At the end of it, he had seen life in its many facets, met all kinds of people, including some of the most extra ordinary 'yogis' whose outward eccentricities concealed the sublimity of their spiritual attainments. His body, mind and soul had been tempered like steel in the crucible of austerities, but the acme of his 'sadhana' was not reached until he went to Shirdi for a 'darshan' of Sai Baba's samadhi. It was that historic day, 29th August 1936, which changed the course of his life. Sai Baba took possession of Narasimha Swamiji. His mind became still and he was face to face with the Master who had given up his physical body eighteen years earlier.

Narasimha Swamiji was granted 'Realization' then and there. He became an evangelist and spread the message of Sai Baba all over the country. He brought out Sai Baba from the narrow confines of Shirdi and spread his message all over the country.

Narasimha Swamiji searched for his Sadguru, discovered him and shared with us all the grace he received from his Sadguru. This, briefly, is the story of his life.

Dr.Vijayakumar is renowned for his prolific writings on Sai Baba and is widely read by devotees all over India. He is a research scholar who revels in assiduous collection of data, without leaving out even minute details and embellishes them with an easy style of presentation. He has brought out a vivid picture of Swamiji's personality and a lucid presentation of his life in this book.

Narasimha Swamiji's life is a spiritual triumph. At the sight of that holy face shining like the Full Moon, our hearts overflow with Divine joy. This is our humble prayer to Sri Narasimha Swamiji – "Oh Gurudev, may this little offering of ours, dedicated to you in the intoxication of our love and reverence meet with your gracious approval! May your merciful blessings be upon us!"

Bangalore

15th March 2007

R. Seshadri

President

Sri Sai Spiritual Centre

Bangalore 560028

Author's submission

I was employed at Kil-Kotagiri in the Nilgiris District of Tamil Nadu during 1986-88. From the living room of my residence which was on a hilltop, I could see in distant plains the course of Bhavani river. Whenever I used to look at the course of river Bhavani, I used to have visions of Narasimha Swamiji. When I mentioned this to Sri O.K.Varada Rao, the first Secretary of the All India Sai Samaj, he was overwhelmed with joy and expressed that I am indeed under the benign grace of Narasimha Swamiji. He narrated a number of his personal experiences with Narasimha Swamiji, which created an indelible impression in my mind. Sri Varada Rao looked upon my wife, Seetha as his foster daughter and used to call me affectionately 'Alludu' in Telugu, which means son-in-law.

Sri T.A. Ram Nathen of Kolkata had earlier sent me a book on Sri Narasimha Swamiji written by Sri P.S. Varadaraja Iyer. I also had a copy of the book 'Apostle of Sai Baba – Life of Sri Narasimha Swamiji' written by my Gurudev, Sri Radhakrishna Swamiji.

Armed with some details on Sri Narasimha Swamiji's life and Mission, I delivered a few lectures on Sri Narasimha Swamiji's life from 1989 onwards at Bangalore, Chennai, Delhi, Kolkata, Coimbatore, Mumbai, Pune etc., However, a concrete idea to publish a comprehensive biography on Sri Narasimha Swamiji came up after I delivered a lecture on Sri Narasimha Swamiji on 21.8.2006 at Sri Sai Spiritual Centre, Bangalore in connection with his 132nd birth anniversary. Volunteers of Sri Sai Spiritual Centre came forward to bear the expenses for publishing a book on Narasimha Swamiji and distributing it free to devotees on the ensuing 50th Aradhana day on 7th October 2006. Although I was diffident to take up this task, Sri Narasimha Swamiji made me an instrument and through me he himself wrote his biography in Kannada and the book was dedicated to his lotus feet on 7th October 2006. Those devotees who did not know Kannada made a specific request that I should write an English version to cater to a wider circle of devotees. Again with Swamiji's grace, this work *Sri Narasimha Swami: Apostle of Shirdi Sai Baba* is now being dedicated to our Parama Guru.

I am indebted to Sri R. Seshadri (President, Sri Sai Spiritual Centre, Bangalore) for penning a scholarly foreword, Sri M.S. Jothi Raghavan (Secretary, S.S.S.C) for the affectionate reminders, Sri Gopinath and Smt. Indira of Saipadananda Graphics for printing the 1st Edition, Sri S. K. Kapur (Ex. Hon Secretary, Sri Sai Bhakta Samaj, Lodhi Road, Delhi) and Dr. Rabinder Nath Kakarya for providing rare photographs of Swamiji for the 2nd edition.

The credit of publishing both the English and Hindi version of this book in an attractive, systematic form goes to Sri Surinder Kumar Ghai, Managing Director of Sterling Publishers Pvt. Ltd., New Delhi. His enriched experience and expertise in this field yielded all the support I needed. I express my warmest of regards to him also.

As long as Sai Baba's name is there in this universe, Narasimha Swamiji will be remembered. Whenever we see Sai Baba, we should see Sri Narasimha Swamiji in one eye and Sri Radhakrishna Swamiji in the other.

It was characteristic of Sri Narasimha Swamiji that he rarely spoke of himself and his early life and he did not encourage devotees to raise the topic. But his biographer has to write about his early life too, otherwise the book will be incomplete. What I discovered about Swamiji after research and talks with some of his veteran devotees like the late Sri T.A.Ram Nathen, late Sri O.K.Varada

Rao, late Sri T.Kesava Rao, Smt.Sita Shri and Sri R.Radhakrishnan, who apart from answering my questions, placed at my disposal a number of back issues of 'Sai Sudha', some souvenirs and a few letters, it was indeed a new dimension to the life and Mission of this divine evangelist of Sai Baba.

To those who seek 'the peace that passeth understanding' this book *Sri Narasimha Swami: Apostle of Shirdi Sai Baba* will be interesting as well as inspiring. The road traversed by Sri Narasimha Swamiji was long and hard, but he has shown us Sai Baba.

The life of Sri Narasimha Swamiji is a beacon light to all seekers of Truth. If this book helps any seeker to understand Sri Narasimha Swamiji's immortal and immortalizing message, I shall deem my labours amply rewarded.

Bangalore   **Dr. G.R.Vijayakumar**

Contents

Dedication   5

Introductory Note   7

Foreword   9

Author's submission   13

Part-1: The Early Years of Our Gurudev   19

    Birth and childhood   21

    Childhood in Salem   25

    Youth and Marriage   29

    Public life   31

    The turning point   36

Part-II: In Quest of God   40

    At Sringeri   41

    With Ramana Bhagawan   43

    At Siddharudashram   47

    Pandarapur   49

    From 1932 to March 1934   52

    At Sakori   58

Part-III: God Realization   63

    Face to face with the Master   64

    Early days of Sai Prachar   67

    Baba himself favours the movement 70

The only aim   75
With a repulsive leper   78
Part-IV: **Narasimha Swamiji's Mission**
80
Early days of his Mission   81
Lockets and calendars   86
Lectures and discourses   89
Meeting the disciple   92
Efficient system for Sai Prachar   99
Swamiji's Mahasamadhi   108
After Mahasamadhi   112
Comrades in Baba's service   117
Epilogue   120
Part-V: Some Reminiscences   123
Concept of surrender by *Sri Narasimha Swamiji*   124
Shubra Marga (My first meeting with
Sri Narasimha Swamiji at Ooty) by
    Sri Radhakrishna Swamiji   127
Some Reminiscences   129
Seek the Light within! (Sri Narasimha Swamiji's
    message to readers)   134
Guru's Grace   135

Part-1

The Early Years of Our Gurudev

A medium frame, covered in a long shirt, and a single dhoti going round the waist like a lungi, broad forehead, fronting a head almost bald, carries a cloth bag that comes down from the shoulder and walks briskly along. The bag holds small packets of *udhi* from Shirdi, copies of pocket size 'Ashtotharam' on Sai Baba compiled by him and pictures of Sai Baba in card size – these are his gifts to the sick and needy that accost him for relief and the gifts work wonders. As he passes on the udhi he mutters – "Sai Baba Paripoorna Siddhirasthu". This great soul is worthy of remembrance by any Sai devotee forever.

Prior to 1940, all over India, hardly anyone knew about Sai Baba or heard of the place 'Shirdi'. But today we find temples of Sai Baba in nooks and corners of the country. Associations of Sai devotees, Satsangs, Samajs are in plenty. Many have given Baba's name to their children. Many shops, institutions, industries bear Sai Baba's name. It was Sri Narasimha Swamiji's pioneering efforts of Sai Prachar from village to village, city to city and making individual house visits to take the message Sai Baba out of the small hamlet of Shirdi in the remote corner of Maharashtra to all over the country and even abroad. For this purpose, every Sai devotee should be ever grateful for the strenuous efforts of Sri Narasimha Swamiji from 1936 till he attained 'Mahasamadhi' in 1956. When we offer obeisance to Sai Maharaj, our foremost 'Pranams' should be to Sri Narasimha Swamiji.

Who is Sri Narasimha Swamiji? Who are his parents? How did he live? How did he realize Sai Baba? What are his efforts to distribute the treasure of 'Sai Baba's grace' to one and all? An attempt is made in all humility to tell the fascinating story of this messenger of Sai Baba in the following pages.

Birth and childhood

Bhavani in the Erode district of Tamil Nadu, has been known over the centuries as a place of pilgrimage. Thousands of devotees from all over South India visit Bhavani round the year to seek the grace of Lord Sangameswar and Goddess Bhavani here. The town is situated at the confluence of three rivers – Kaveri, Bhavani and Gupthagamini. It is popularly called the 'Triveni Sangam' of Tamil Nadu.

A Brahmin couple belonging to 'Srivatsa Gothram', Venkatagiri Iyer and Angachiammal, offered daily prayers at the temple of Lord Sangameswar and Bhavani for the gift of a son. Angachiammals's faith in Lord Sangameswar was reinforced by a chance visit of a 'Sadhu' to her home. Knowing her desire, the Sadhu asked her to visit Lord Narasimha at Sholangar. Departing, he told her that Lord Narasimha of Sholangar would definitely bless her with a son.

Soon after a trip to Sholangar, the most cherished desire of that pious woman was fulfilled. Angachiammal became pregnant and the couple was happily looking forward to the arrival of the baby. The D-day was on 'Sravan Panchami', August 21, 1874. On that day, at dusk, around 6.15 pm - at the time when cattle would return home, the auspicious time considered 'Godhuli Muhurtham'; a son was born to Angachiammal under most unusual circumstances. At the moment of his birth, she was walking towards the cattle shed in the spacious compound of her house. The child, who was later to be known as Sri Narsimha Swamiji, took his birth without warning and, with a suddenness and agility that is rare in such cases, even before somebody's assistance could be summoned.

The very circumstances of his birth are thus symbolic of the man, who, with characteristic agility and energy, was destined to wander the wide-open world; indeed, he was born in the open – in the lap of Mother Earth. The unbound, free soul was greeted by the vast expanse of the sky above. The departing rays of sun had just spread themselves over the lush green landscape, weaving varied patterns of light and shade through the trees. The nearby Bhavani river played melodious music as it flowed gently along the bank and the tall coconut trees swinging their leaves gently, seemed to lend graceful rhythm by the gentle swaying of their fronds.

The child was welcomed as a gift from God. He was weighed in gold and silver, which were then offered to Lord Narasimha of Sholangar in grateful acknowledgement of His grace. He was named Narasimha as per the wishes of his mother Angachiammal, even though the father wanted to name him as 'Ramanathan' as the child was born with the same star as that of Lord Sri Ramachandra. That is, 'Punarvasu – 4th padam' of 'Kataka' Rasi. The other famed personalities who share this star are Adi Sankaracharya and Ramana Bhagawan. At the time of his birth, auspicious planets were exalting and since three auspicious planets were in the Lagna, the family astrologer predicted a bright future to the boy, who would evolve to be a great man.

He was born in a rich and pious family. His father was a second grade Pleader and owned a large area of land. The family had a big house situated in a beautiful quiet spot on the banks of the river Bhavani. Green paddy fields and coconut grooves afforded an ideal landscape to the place.

As time passed, Narasimha grew into a fine, handsome boy, well built, agile and intelligent, with deep-set eyes that were immediately captivating. From his infancy, he was joyful, imaginative, clever and mischievous too. The child was different from other boys. A teacher used to come home and teach the alphabets. Narasimha would gather all the children around him, play jokes on them and make them do things. Right from his early days he was a leader. He liked to rule but never to be ruled. He would never pick a quarrel, but if it came to fighting, he was a ruthless opponent. He would not tolerate any injustice and, with his fiery nature, he could be easily roused. He never allowed himself to be fooled by anyone. He was of a very independent nature. Strangely Narasimha had no close friends and hence no attachments either outside or within the family. His mother pampered him; yet he was not spoiled. All loved him, and his playfulness and mischief endeared him to everyone. He was always full of vigour and looked rather too mature for his age.

Three years after Narasimha was born, that is in 1877, Angachiammal gave birth to another son. The younger son was named 'Lakshmana'. Unfortunately he lived for a short period. When the second son was three years old, that is somewhere in 1880, some miscreants kidnapped him, robbed him of his ornaments and murdered him. The younger son's death had deeply affected the parents.

One year prior to Lakshmana's death that is in 1879 the parents were in for another shock. The whole family along with farmers and other workmen had assembled on the banks of river Bhavani for a special 'Pooja' on a 'Sankranthi' day. The five-year old child Narasimha while playing slipped into the river and would have met a watery grave, but for the timely intervention of a farmer who jumped into the river and saved the young child.

Venkatagiri Iyer and Angachiammal sought the opinion of their family astrologer. He predicted that Narasimha escaped an untimely death and hence would live for over eighty years. He advised change of place to the parents. He also predicted that Narasimha will be a great person of eminence and would guide the destinies of thousands of persons. But in the same stroke, the astrologer added a tangential remark that there is a possibility of

Narasimha renouncing his family to become a 'Sadhu' later on. This was indeed an unexpected prediction for the parents as they had already lost their second son and if the first son became a 'sadhu' their lineage would snap. This was quite was unthinkable to them.

The couple prayed for a divine intervention. Angachiammal was thirty-six years old and at her earnest request, at the temple of Lord Sangameswar and Goddess Bhavani, she and Venkatagiri Iyer took the vows of celibacy for the rest of their lives, so that Narasimha would take up a family life, when he grew up.

Based on the family astrologer's advice, Venkatagiri Iyer disposed of his house and a great portion of his landed property at Bhavani, retaining only few acres of paddy fields and coconut groves and decided to migrate to Salem – forty kilometers away from Bhavani.

Venkatagiri Iyer changed his residence to Hastinampatti – an upcoming extension in Salem town. He continued his practice as a second grade Pleader at Salem.

Childhood in Salem

The child Narasimha was admitted to a school at Salem. He had already learnt the alphabets and other basics at Bhavani from a teacher who visited his house daily for this purpose.

Narasimha's mental make-up and inner spirit were vastly different from those of other children of his age. He was highly intelligent and extremely good in his studies. Theories and dogmas did not interest him but he could be convinced only by actual observation and direct experience. He liked to explore the unknown. The accounts of far-off places and countries fascinated him and made him restless. Ambitious and adventure loving, he had a desire to become a hero. Being physically and intellectually far more precocious than other boys of his age, he found his schoolmates dull. His impatient nature could not tolerate sluggishness or slovenliness of any kind. He feared that he, too, would stagnate in their company, and to him stagnation was like death.

The parents, Venkatagiri Iyer and Angachiammal had brought up the child Narasimha in a suitable religious atmosphere and had inculcated high social responsibility. The parents were large-hearted and known for their generosity. Even at Bhavani, Angachiammal used to distribute the first crop of mangoes, coconuts and other fruits grown in their garden and the paddy harvested in their fields to neighbours, friends and their bungalow servants and retained a quantity adequate for their personal use. In his later life, Sri Narasimha Swamiji used to recall this incident and say - "I learnt voluntary social obligation from my mother."

Narasimha's father, Venkatagiri Iyer, was a very learned and deeply religious man. At night, he would gather all the family members, friends and neighbours around him and read out portions from epics like Ramayana, Mahabharata, Bhagavata etc., On festival days, he would invite saints and scholars and arrange their religious discourses at his house. He also used to hold ballets, which depicted the story of the epics like Mahabharata and Ramayana. Narasimha had many opportunities to witness these mythological shows, in which characteristics of mystic sages and yogis interested him the most. The impressionable Narasimha admired their powers, their vision, their wisdom and above all their command even over the rulers and kings who prostrated before them. He desired to be one of them, that is, a 'Sadhu', without knowing the exact meaning of the word.

Venkatagiri Iyer was free from superstition. He did not hesitate to engage even Muslim singers to sing devotional songs in his house. "If there be any element of purity in me, it has been inherited from my father", in his later life Sri Narasimha Swamiji once confided in his devotees.

His mother's influence on Narasimha was immense. She regularly used to sing devotional songs to her son in order to nurture his religious sentiments. If any sage or saint visited Salem, invariably Venkatagiri Iyer and Angachiammal would be the first to invite him to their house. Sri Narasimha Bharathi Swamiji, Jagadguru Sankaracharya of Sringeri and Sorakkai Swamiji who lived near Kalahasthi are the two great sages who deeply impressed young Narasimha. The Jagadguru Sankaracharya of Sringeri, Sri Narasimha Bharathi Swamiji, who was looked upon as Adi Guru Sankaracharya reborn, had a large and diverse following and in the very first meeting, he blessed the child Narasimha and gently stroked him on the cheeks. Soon after this, Sri Narasimha Bharathi Swamiji walked away from that place. The child Narasimha looked at him and observed that the Jagadguru was striding fast with his feet hardly touching the ground. The boy felt a strange, magnetic spell, particularly from his powerful eyes, the impact of which remained with him. "This incident," in his later life Sri Narasimha Swamiji says, "is so vivid that I just cannot forget it. It will ever remain with me as a treasure."

In 1882, eight-year-old Narasimha had his 'Brahmopadesham'. Sri Nataraja Vadyar who stayed close by taught the young boy the rituals of *Sandhyavandana*. Having been initiated into *Gayathri Japam* by his father Venkatagiri Iyer, performing *Sandhyavandana* three times a day and doing *Gayathri Japam* became a part of life for Narasimha. Soon after this, the boy was enrolled in a *Veda Patashala* to learn *Rudra*, *Chamaka*, *Sri Sukta* and *Purusha Sukta*. A friendly neighbour, Alamelamma trained the young boy to recite *Vishnu Sahasranama*, *Lalitha Sahsranama* and other divine chanting. Every day by 4 pm Alamelamma used to call out for Narasimha in Tamil – "*Kanna – Sloka sollu vaa*", the boy invariably used to run with all enthusiasm to Alamelamma's house to learn reciting Sahasranamas.

Angachiammal directed Narasimha to water the tulsi plant and feed a cow every day before taking food. When Narasimha wanted to know the reason, she said. "It is not proper to take food before offering it to others".

Angachiammal used to give alms to beggars whenever they approached her. One day, seeing her give alms to a well-built beggar, Narasimha protested that she was being kind to a man who did not deserve it. In reply, his mother said, "Narsimha, who are we to judge who is worthy and who is unworthy? All who come to us for help are God in human forms. So we must provide whatever help is within our means". She was also very considerate towards the so-called untouchables and it was from her that Narsimha learnt that "he who gives is a God, but he who withholds is a devil". Angachiammal's utterances taught Narsimha that service performed in the right spirit of 'karma yoga' becomes 'worship of Shiva in the Jiva', which is one of the most effective means of self-purification and God-realization.

Narsimha's mother used to serve neighbours in times of need. On one occasion when a neighbour was indisposed, she went to cook for them after having finished her own cooking at home. Disapproving of this, Narasimha said, "Mother, you are selfish. Why didn't you cook for them first and then do our cooking?" His mother replied, "If I cooked their food first, it would get cold by the time they ate it". The answer went straight into Narasimha's heart.

The large hearted Angachiammal was an effective Guru to her son. In his later life, Sri Narsimha Swamiji hardly talked about himself; he occasionally used to speak of his mother's influence on him.

After finishing schooling at Salem, Narsimha left for Madras for further studies – first intermediate, later for BA and Law degrees.

Youth and Marriage

Narasimha Iyer joined the Madras Christian College as a student of Intermediate class. He distinguished himself as a brilliant student. He was guided by his mother's advice – "I am the third". That is, God is foremost in his life, next others and then the third one is himself.

When he completed his Junior Intermediate examination in 1890 and came home for summer vacation, his wedding bells were ringing. Venkatagiri Iyer and Angachiammal were anxious to have their son married and settled in life. On an auspicious day, Seethalakshmi, the only daughter of Kallakurchi Vaidyanatha Iyer and Shanta – a rich landlord family of Kumarapalayam near Erode, became the life partner of Narasimha Iyer. At that time, Narasimha Iyer was sixteen years old and Seethalakshmi was ten years of age.

Narasimha Iyer went back to his studies at the Madras Christian College. He came under the magnetic spell of Jesus Christ and deeply studied the Bible. His relatives were scared about his fascination towards Christianity and were even afraid that he may get himself converted to Christianity. However the youthful Narasimha Iyer was more attracted by the tenets of universal love and brotherhood practised by Jesus Christ rather than getting converted to Christianity.

From his childhood days, Narasimha Iyer's entire family was devoted to Sorakkai Swamiji – a mystic saint who lived near

Kalahasthi. Narasimha Iyer had met this saint on many occasions along with his parents.

After completing his Intermediate course with a distinction, Narasimha Iyer continued in the Madras Christian College to obtain his BA degree. He was an adept public speaker and had won laurels in several debates and elocution competitions. Though he was a forceful speaker even in normal conversation, he was nice to everyone.

Depending upon the situation, Narasimha Iyer was an outspoken person. One instance during his college days is worthy of mention here. At the Madras Christian College, he used to avail of the Library facilities quite frequently. One summer day, feeling very hot in the library room he removed his shirt. The library attendant objected to this and when Narasimha Iyer refused to listen to him the matter was reported to the Librarian, who happened to be an Englishman. The Librarian called him to his room and asked him if he knew what good manners were. Narasimha Iyer firmly replied that he did, saying, "In our country, we do not think it good for one to remain seated and keep another standing." The librarian was taken aback and offered him a chair. Narasimha Iyer then added, "In our country we remove shirts during hot weather because it is healthy and convenient." The librarian could not refute this logic.

He successfully completed BA in distinction and joined the Madras Law College to pursue a legal degree. In 1895, Narasimha Iyer returned to Salem after obtaining a Law degree.

Public life

Narasimha Iyer straightaway joined the Bar and began to practise at Salem from 1895. The rare legal acumen and persuasive eloquence he showed in conducting his cases brought Narasimha Iyer phenomenal success at the bar, large clientele, princely income and powerful influence. Very soon he became one of the leaders of the Bar.

As an advocate, Narasimha Iyer was very calm while presenting his case and arguments in court. But he would not hesitate to needle and irritate the lawyer on the other side to make him lose his trend of thought.

By nature and temperament, he was always sympathetic to the masses. Considering the high cost of litigation and the ruin it brought in the end to both the parties, Narasimha Iyer used to conduct a 'Panchayat court' in his house, allowed the lawyers to put up the respective cases of the parties and dealt out justice cheaply and agreeably to both the parties.

At the Bar, Narasimha Iyer had a good company. Among his prominent contemporaries as members of the Bar at Salem were, Sri C.Rajagopalachari, who later on became the last Governor General of India, Sri Sundaram Chetty, who later on became a Judge of the Madras High court, Sri Vijayaraghavachari, who later on presided over the All-India Congress session at Nagpur in 1920 and Sri Muthukrishna Iyer, a Bar-at-Law and a freedom fighter.

Not content with acquiring fame and amassing wealth as a lawyer, Narasimha Iyer interested himself in all the public activities and movements of the day. As elsewhere, so in politics, his involvement brought him to a position of importance and leadership seemed to come to him naturally. In 1902, he was elected as a member of the Salem Municipal Council. He was also elected as a Director of the Salem Co-operative Bank.

Salem wanted an efficient administrator. The integrity, unassuming simplicity and helpful nature of Narasimha Iyer won for him the esteem and regard of the public. In 1904 he was called upon to serve the Salem Municipality as its Chairman. He held this position for a record seventeen years and earned immense popularity. Concurrently he was also elected as the Chairman of the Salem Co-operative Bank.

Narasimha Iyer became an active member of the Literary Society where he used to play tennis and billiards. However, on the stroke of six every evening, he would stop playing and go home saying, "the honest man's hour has come, I must go". Friends, who were intrigued at this, later found out that the 'honest man' went home at that hour regularly to perform his evening pooja and offer prayers.

In politics he was an admirer and follower of the firebrand leader, Sri Bala Gangadhar Tilak, and was considered an extremist. This made him very popular and in 1914, he was elected to represent the districts – Salem, Coimbatore and Nilgiris in the Madras Legislative Council. He was also elected to the new Council established under the Montague-Chelmsford reforms. He continued to be a member of the Legislative Council till 1920 and, as a member of the Indian National Congress, he vigorously presented the national viewpoint on all issues that came up for consideration before the Council.

In the days before the Montague-Chelmsford reforms, the Governor of Madras would preside over the Council. On one occasion, Narasimha Iyer addressed the Council in Tamil and this perplexed the Governor and other members.

It was Narasimha Iyer who started the much-talked-of mass contact. As a rule, in the olden days, those who entered the Legislature did not submit to democratic control. However, Narasimha Iyer, after every session of the Council, would inform his constituents of all that took place in the Council and his own part therein. Others follow this example now.

He used to visit Madras for attending the Legislature sessions and he became a prominent figure in the public life of Madras also. He was frequently invited to deliver lectures on current problems and invariably they drew large attendance. He was well known for presenting his points briefly and clearly in a pleasing style and the quotations from English literature and Sanskrit works.

Narasimha Iyer had an extraordinary knowledge of men and things. In fact, for a long time after he set up law practice, he was an examiner for the Madras University in Roman History and Greek History. It was rare that one combined in oneself so much knowledge and saintly traits.

As he gained his popularity in public life, his family had also grown. Narasimha Iyer and Seethalakshmi had five children – eldest son Venkataraman followed by daughters Rajalakshmi and Saradambal, second son Jayaraman and the youngest daughter Savithri. By 1916, Venkataraman, Rajalakshmi and Saradambal were married and only the younger two – Jayaraman and Savithri were with the parents.

It may be mentioned in passing, that while living in Salem in the midst of his busy professional and public engagements, Narasimha Iyer found time to perform 'sandhya' three times a day, Tulsi Pooja regularly, daily recitation of sahasranamas, Go-pooja on Fridays and also to visit periodically Sorakkai Swamiji, a mystic who lived near Kalahasthi and the Jagadguru Sankaracharya of Sringeri. He also used to lead bhajan singers on every Saturday evenings at Sri Lakshminarayan temple near his residence by singing the Brindavan *kirtanas* composed by him.

By 1915 he had reached the peak of his power, popularity and wealth. He had built a big bungalow in Sivaswamipuram extension of Salem. His bungalow was one of the very few in Salem, which had electricity. With all facilities like car, bungalow, servants etc., Narasimha Iyer led a princely life. Right through he pursued a policy of service and sacrifice. To him politics did not mean the gateway to a career or profession. Others who worked with him blossomed in free India as Ministers, Governors, Ambassadors or Chairmen of Commissions carrying perquisites and profits.

By 1915, Dr.Annie Besant had organised the Home Rule League to agitate for the freedom of India from the British administration. Narasimha Iyer worked with Dr.Annie Besant by going round the Madras Presidency on lecture tours. Madras Presidency was then far bigger in size than the present Tamil Nadu. Narasimha Iyer was our first national leader to conceive the idea of mass contact and visit the rural areas and create mass political awakening. The Congress Working Committee adopted this later on to cover the entire nation.

Meanwhile, the First World War was going on. E.S.Montague was the Secretary of State for India and Lord Chelmsford was the Viceroy of India. These two persons had worked out the famous Montague-Chelmsford reforms for India to be implemented after the war was over. The war-torn public of England were preparing for an election in 1917 to get a Government that would bring the war to a close. Our national leaders hoped to persuade the Liberals who were contesting the General Elections in England to make granting of political independence to India an election issue of their party. It was felt that only those who had wisdom and experience in our national work could by their eloquent pleading, create a favourable impression among the Liberals, on our behalf. In order to work out their plan in England, a delegation of three members comprising Narasimha Iyer, George Joseph and Manjeri Rama Iyer was constituted. This delegation sailed by the Cape route to avoid observation at the Suez Canal. The British war cabinet got scent of their move and, being aware of their capacity to influence British public opinion, had them arrested at Gibraltar and deported them back to India, after fifteen days' detention.

In 1920, Narasimha Iyer was re-elected to the Legislative Council, but resigned in pursuance of the Non-Co-operation Movement started by Mahatma Gandhi.

With all these political activities, Narasimha Iyer was also engaged in carrying out extensive repairs to the Lakshminarayan Temple at Salem and building an extension to the temple.

An epidemic of plague struck the world in 1917 and over forty lakh people died. Narasimha Iyer's mother was the first casualty to this epidemic of plague at Salem. Deeply struck by his mother's death, within a few months, Narasimha Iyer had to face another bereavement. In the early 1918, his father Venkatagiri Iyer breathed his last due to an attack of cholera.

Narasimha Iyer took these bereavements in his stride and continued to engage himself fully in his political, social and religious activities.

The turning point

While still at the peak of his power, prestige and popularity, Narasimha Iyer decided in 1921, following a series of domestic calamities to give up his lucrative legal practice and also to withdraw from political and social activities. It was at such a juncture in Narasimha Iyer's life that providence took a hand and decided to take him away from worldly activities. The means chosen for this withdrawal was a terrible domestic tragedy.

It was the last week of April 1921. Children were at home as it was summer vacation for schools. Narasimha Iyer was performing the annual ceremony of his late mother. Having completed all ceremonial rites, Narasimha Iyer was preparing for feeding the priests. The leaves were spread and the food served and the priests were about to start partaking their food. At that moment Narasimha Iyer's children – 15-year old, younger son Jayaraman and 13-year old youngest daughter Savithri – while playing, had accidentally fallen into a half-dug well in their compound and had met a watery grave. One of the bungalow servants came and whispered this tragic news into the ears of Narasimha Iyer, as the Brahmins were about to start partaking their food. Even though it was like a torpedo hitting him, Narasimha Iyer controlled his emotions with a great presence of mind, did not reveal the sad demise of his children to the priests assembled there and requested the priests to proceed with their food and complete the formalities of his mother's ceremony. After everything was over, he quietly proceeded to the backyard of his bungalow to see his dead children.

The death of two children in one stroke was like a thunderbolt. He was 47 years old at that time. He had not expected to be treated in this way by the heavens for whatever he had done for the public good. This tragedy could have made any other man go off his head and swear against God.

Why should this happen to him? What then is the meaning of life? Condolence and consolation, he received from various quarters. But none was found competent to give him satisfactory answers to his problems.

It took some years for the paroxysm of grief to subside. He had to gain control over himself. He settled down and pondered over the situation. He had educated his other son and helped him live on his income. His surviving daughters, Rajalakshmi and Saradambal, had already been married decently. He was left alone in the wide world with his sorrowing wife.

Narasimha Iyer realized that the one who gave him the terrible blow was none other than God Himself. Therefore, the tragedy that struck him must be intended to produce, eventually, beneficial effects on Narasimha Iyer and, through him, on the people at large. Through this instrument Narasimha Iyer, who was a *Grihastha* (family man) in full possession of the powers of his body and mind, was turned away from mundane activities so that he might engage in spiritual pursuits for the larger good. Narasimha Iyer took an irrevocable decision to take to spiritual pursuit and to serve God and humanity through devotion and knowledge. In the second volume of his masterpiece 'Life of Sai Baba', Sri Narasimha Swamiji throws considerable light on this turning point in his life.

Agitating for Home Rule. Asserting the rights of people and educating the people about their rights and participating in political and legislative activities was, no doubt, public service. But while there was enough workers and more were coming into the political field who were able, young and energetic and were suited for political activity, there was an imperative need for service in the spiritual field which was starved of true workers, because men with the adamantine character and total dedication necessary for true spiritual service were hard to find.

Even as the bodies of his little children were being taken out of the well, even as his benumbed mind and stricken heart were beginning to recover from shock and sorrow, Narasimha Iyer realized that providence was conveying a message to him through this tragedy and directing him to concentrate himself on the service of mankind, breaking the shackles of political and social activity and domestic environment.

The final goal, that is, realization of Self and God, though but dimly perceived at this time, became clear soon enough and Narasimha Iyer knew that he had to take a 180-degree turn and proceed in a direction exactly the opposite of the one he had been pursuing thus far.

His wife Seethalakshmi was unable to bear the loss of her children and ultimately passed away in 1922. So Narasimha Iyer was left all alone in a big bungalow.

Narasimha Iyer resolved to make an absolute renunciation of everything he was connected with till then and to lead a secluded and consecrated life. He relinquished his interests in his property. He had already resigned the membership of the Legislature in 1920 in response to the Non-Co operation Movement of Mahatma Gandhi and ceased to participate in political and other controversial public affairs. The final symbolic act was the return of his 'Vakil Sanad' to the High Court in 1925.

His withdrawal from the temporal life was orderly and gradual so that his disengagement caused the least dislocation to others. Finally, after completing the work connected with the Lakshminarayana Temple, he left home and family life in search of spiritual guidance and a Guru in accordance with the advice of the *Kula Acharya* and other elders.

Narasimha Iyer possessed those qualities and qualifications necessary for a 'sadhaka' to receive lessons in spiritual wisdom and training in spiritual discipline. He had led a clean life and had also a keen spiritual perception. Narasimha Iyer had drunk deep of the fountain of 'Prastanatraya', which in one word, stands for Bhagavadgita, Brahmasutras and the Upanishads, and which is the source of Vedanta. He knew Viveka Chudamani and Yoga Vasishta. He had read Valmiki Ramayana, Mahabharata and Srimad Bhagavatam. He could recite according to correct phonetics and rhythm, *Purusha Sooktam, Sri Sooktam. Durga Sooktam* and *Shanti Panchakam.* He was also well versed in the New Testament, Shakespeare, Tennyson, Wordsworth etc.,

With this background, he distributed his wealth among his children, cut off all his family ties and left Salem in September 1925 as a mendicant.

At last, the bird flew away from its cage. He loved freedom dearly. The bonds of family love could not bind his free spirit. He walked away penniless, but, strangely, this did not worry him. When God pulls one towards him, as though by a string tied to the heart, it becomes his responsibility to protect that person. Narasimha Iyer experienced this from the time he left Salem.

Narasimha Iyer was brought up in the orthodox tradition. Even in the midst of his busy secular life, he never neglected the performance of his *Nitya Karma* (daily rituals like *Sandhyavandana, Gayatri Japam,* ancestor worship etc.,)

Part-II

In Quest of God

At Sringeri

Narasimha Iyer had two options before him, after he gave up his family ties.

The first one was to go over to the Ashram of Sorakkai Swamiji, a mystic who lived near Kalahasthi or take up *Sanyas* from his *Kula Guru* the Jagadguru Sri Shankaracharya of Sringeri. Since by then, Sorakkai Swamiji had cast off his mortal coil, Narsimha Iyer decided to go over to Sringeri in September 1925. Jagadguru Sri Narasimha Bharathi Mahaswamigal who had blessed Narasimha Iyer as a school boy, had attained 'Mahasamadhi' in 1912 itself and Sri Chandrasekhara Bharathi Mahaswamigal had succeeded him as the Pontiff.

At present traveling from one place to another is easy. But in 1925, the situation was different. Travel from Salem to Sringeri – a stretch of over 400 km was a Herculean task. Earlier, Narasimha Iyer used to visit Sringeri in his personal car. Now that he was a mendicant and had left Salem penniless, one can understand how much hardship Narasimha Iyer would have faced in reaching Sringeri.

The authorities of the Shankar Mutt at Sringeri were pleasantly surprised when on a fine morning in October 1925, Narasimha Iyer landed in Sringeri. They were anxious at his stony silence and the mute manner in which he participated in the religious functions of the mutt. After spending three to four months in this manner, Narasimha Iyer poured out his problems to the Jagadguru

Shankaracharya Sri Chandrasekhara Bharathi Mahaswamigal and requested him to initiate him into *Sanyas* at the Shankar Mutt.

Jagadguru Shankaracharya was known for his clairvoyant vision. He must have discerned in his clairvoyant vision the prominent role Narasimha Iyer was going to play by working for the spiritual uplift of the world. The rigid discipline and the limited sphere in which an initiated monk should function afforded little scope for what was expected of Narasimha Iyer. Accordingly, the Shankaracharya initiated him to chant *Panchakshari* mantra, *Om Nama Shivaya*, and directed him to go over to Tiruvannamalai and to join Ramana.

From now onwards it is appropriate to call Narasimha Iyer, Narasimha Swamiji, as Jagadguru Sri Shankarachaya Swamigal initiated him into the *Panchakshari* mantram.

At that time, Ramana was little known outside Tiruvannamalai, but had a small band of devotees and was living at Skandashram on the hill, a little above the base. He was known among devotees as 'Brahmana Swami'.

With Ramana Bhagawan

Tiruvannamalai is a highly sanctified place. Here, Lord Parameswara Himself is in the form of a mountain and blessing the devotees. In this holy place, a number of *siddhas*, sages and sadhus have sought spiritual recluse. It is authoritatively claimed that if the very name Tiruvannamalai were uttered, one would be emancipated from the cycle of births and deaths. Sri Ramana had chosen this holy place as his abode. Narasimha Swamiji arrived in Tiruvannamalai in January 1926.

After visiting the Lord Arunachaleswara temple and seeking the Lord's blessings, Narasimha Swamiji went in search of 'Brahmana Swami' at Skandashram on the slopes of the hill. He paid his obeisance to Ramana Maharishi and submitted to him the directions given by Jagadguru Shankaracharya of Sringeri and requested him for spiritual guidance. Ramana Maharishi showed him a cave, which was behind him and directed Narasimha Swamiji to meditate in that cave on Self-enquiry – 'who am I?'

Ramana Maharishi held that happiness came from within as a 'subjective realization of the mind', though many had misunderstood that it depended on external conditions. By wisely adapting to changing conditions and environment one might preserve a balanced mind. Ramana's answer to any problem was invariably to direct the person concerned, to trace the source of the problem and ask – 'who is affected? Who am I?'

Narasimha Swamiji fitted within this circle and he benefited by developing awareness within. Ramana Maharishi had composed hymns on Lord Arunachala – Aksharamanimala, Arunachala Stuthi Panchakam and Arunachala Ashtakam. He has summed up his teachings in the verses entitled 'Upadeshasaram'.

Narasimha Swamiji actively took part in the daily routine at Ramanashram like contemplating 'Who am I?' reciting Ramana's compositions and going on 'Giri Pradakshina'. He also came in contact with Mahan Seshadri Swamigal, who used to visit Skandashram quite frequently to meet Ramana Maharishi. Narasimha Swamiji's spiritual 'sadhana' was quite intensive.

Narasimha Swamiji was adept at gathering information and interpretation. He collected all available information from the inmates of the Ramanashram, such as Kavyakanta Ganapathy Sastry and other visitors. He also collected adequate information about Mahan Seshadri Swamigal and had made copious notes on his life. One day, Kuzhumani Narayana Sastry made a casual remark to Narasimha Swamiji about his plan to publish a book on Mahan Seshadri Swamigal. Immediately Narasimha Swamiji handed over the copious notes made by him on Mahan Seshadri Swamigal to Kuzhumani Narayana Sastry and requested him to make use of them while preparing the biography of Mahan Seshadri Swamigal. Kuzhumani Narayana Sastry has acknowledged this contribution of Narasimha Swamiji in his book on Mahan Seshadri Swamigal.

Narasimha Swamiji spent three years at Ramanashram. His mind did not attain quietness. It was as confused as it was at the time when he left Salem in September 1925. Still he had a ray of hope that his mind would become still some day or the other.

In January 1929, Mahan Seshadri Swamigal cast off his mortal coil. Narasimha Swamiji took part in his final rites. Later in February 1929, Justice Sri K.Sundaram Chetty, a Judge of the Madras High Court and an old classmate and later companion of Narasimha Swamiji at the Salem Bar visited Tiruvannamalai. He was surprised to see Narasimha Swamiji among the devotees of Ramana Maharishi. The old friends met at one place after a long time. They reminisced the good old college and professional days. While Justice Sundaram Chetty was taking leave, Narasimha Swamiji handed over the notes he had made on Ramana Bhagawan.

Justice Sundaram Chetty went through the manuscript given by Narasimha Swamiji and he was deeply impressed by it. He wanted to share this benefit with all other spiritual aspirants and as such impressed upon M/S Higginbothams to publish the work in book form.

Narasimha Swamiji's manuscript took the shape of an authoritative biography of Ramana Maharishi under the title 'Self-Realization'. M/S Higginbothams has sales counters in Railway stations, airports, bus stations, and prominent places and within a short period of its publication, Ramana Maharishi's name spread all over the world. Ramana Maharishi, whose value was appreciated and profited by a limited circle, became known by this publication, to a larger number of people. In fact, it opened up the floodgates to devotees and aspirants swarmed to Ramana from all over the globe. In this context, it may be assessed how quick was the intellectual perception of Narasimha Swamiji and also under what a deep debt of gratitude he has placed the world by discovering Ramana Maharishi and making him known everywhere by this biography. Even though hundreds of books on Ramana Maharishi are now available, the first book on him is by Narasimha Swamiji. Somehow, Justice Sri K.Sundaram Chetty published it. In 1931, Ramanashram itself brought out this publication with a foreword by Justice Sri K.Sundaram Chetty. Till date fifteen editions of this book have been brought out and has been translated into several languages.

Life with Ramana Maharishi did contribute to the spiritual enlightenment of Narasimha Swamiji. It was all intellectual practice and if devotion was needed, songs were addressed to Ramana Maharishi. Narasimha Swamiji was thirsting to drink from the pool of juicy devotion to grow his heart alongside his head and he found that he had lost the fervour of 'Bhakti' in which he had made good progress before leaving Salem. So sometime in August 1929, Narasimha Swamiji sought from Ramana Maharishi as to when he would be bestowed with peace of mind. Ramana Maharishi intently looked at Narasimha Swamiji and told him – "I am not your Guru. Your Guru is waiting for you in the North. You will attain Realization from him."

With the permission and blessings of Ramana Maharishi, Narasimha Swamiji left Ramanashram in August 1929 for Western India.

At Siddharudashram

—◆—

Narasimha Swamiji set out in his quest. He had no money in his pocket. As a mendicant he had to walk or travel in a vehicle if someone offered a lift. If somebody offered, he would take food or otherwise he would fast. He did not care about his body. He had left everything to God. His only motto was to go in search of a Guru – a guide to spiritual wisdom and attain God-Realization.

As Narasimha Swamiji left Tiruvannamalai, on the way, a friendly lorry driver offered him a lift and gave him tea and bread. As Narasimha Swamiji mentioned his 'search for a Guru'. The lorry driver offered him a suggestion – "I am going to Hubli. A great saint lives there. His name is Siddharuda Swamiji. He is so powerful that even wild animals like lions and tigers follow his instructions." Narasimha Swamiji was reminded of the lines in *Vishnu Sahasranama* – "Anukulah Satavartah…" etc., where Lord Narayana takes a form to help his devotees. He considered the lorry driver as God coming in that guise to help him. He readily accepted his suggestion and accordingly landed in Hubli by the end of August 1929 to go over to the Ashram of Siddharuda Swamiji.

Siddharuda Swamiji was a great 'Siddha Purusha', whose fame had spread far and wide. Narasimha Swamiji was readily accepted in the ashram. Even though he was reciting Sahasranamas, he had no knowledge of Sanskrit. At Siddarudashram, he learnt Sanskrit from the basics and studied the elements of Vedanta and Yoga. He studied texts on Vedanta like the *Vicharasagara*, the *Panchadashi*, the *Yogavasista* and the *Panchakarana*. He also studied Saivism at Siddharudashram. This gave him the knowledge of the real meaning of the eternal truth, higher than which there could be nothing.

Narasimha Swamiji's knowledge, wisdom, humility were exemplary and soon he became a favourite of Siddharuda Swamiji. One of his companions in the Ashram was Krishna, who later on became Swami Muktananda Maharaj, a disciple of Swami Nityananda who established a magnificent ashram at Ganeshpuri. Siddaruda Swamiji's fascination for Narasimha Swamiji made others jealous of him. They made several attempts to tarnish the image of Narasimha Swamiji and throw him out of the Siddaruda Ashram, as they were afraid of his popularity and the fear that he might be anointed as a successor to Siddharuda Swamiji. All their attempts failed because Siddharuda Swamiji had high regard for Narasimha Swamiji.

Unfortunately, in early 1930, Siddharuda Swamiji attained Mahasamadhi. It became crystal clear to Narasimha Swamiji that he had no place in the Ashram after the demise of Siddharuda Swamiji. So before being expelled from the ashram, he left Siddharudashram on his own.

Pandarapur

Narasimha Swamiji after coming out of Siddharudashram at Hubli again resumed his quest for a Sadguru. Looking forward to meet his Guru in the north, he reached Pandarapur in February 1930.

Meera Bai, Jayadeva, Gauranga and Tukaram have substantially contributed to our devotional literature. But in our vast country there is no town renowned for devotion as Pandarapur, which is resounding with divine name. According to Bhakta Vijayam the trader chanted 'Hari, Hari' as he sold his wares in the market, 'Hari, Hari'- chanted the teacher as he taught, the servants did the same, and the lady of the house acted likewise as her visitors came to her. Even in our age, this town is resounding with Harinam. It is this holy place, which has produced Saint Purandaradasa. The town has been named after Pundarika, to whom the Lord revealed Himself on an 'eet' (brick). The Lord is worshipped as 'Vittal' or 'Vittoba'. Who is not moved by hearing the glory of Vittal as sung by Tukaram in his composition – "Vittala, Vittala, Jai Jai Vittala, Hari Jai Vittala Panduranga"?

Narasimha Swamiji chose a dynamic centre of divine music, for the purpose of cultivating devotion. He stayed in a Dharmashala in Gungadi Galli at Pandharpur. Here he learnt the local language Marathi and the songs mingled with the ecstatic singers and happily spent twenty months during February 1930 and December 1931.

As the days passed, a feeling of inadequacy began to steal over him. He was in Pandarapur to cultivate devotion. But his aim was to find out a Sadguru. A companion sadhu advised Narasimha Swamiji to meet Bapumai – a remarkable lady saint in that area. Bapumai's peculiarities were that she wore an old loincloth, which she would not change for months together, she had long hair, and she carried with her three small sticks tied together with dirty rags. If asked what it all meant, she would reply :- "I have bound together the three 'Gunas' – Sattva, Rajas and Tamas. I am beyond all three." She used to carry a bundle of torn clothes with her. She would ask for a one-paisa coin from everyone and then go round the temple of Vithoba. In the evening she would go to the river Chandrabhaga and throw all the money into the water, saying: "Mother Chandrabhaga, keep all this money safe for me." Thus the Chandrabhaga was her bank!

One day, Narasimha Swamiji saw her in the streets of Pandharpur and followed her. After going some distance, Bapumai turned back to see who was following her.

She asked Swamiji, "Who are you?"

Swamiji said, "A traveller"

"Where are you going?" inquired Bapumai

"I am following you," replied Swamiji.

Bapumai said, "I have no place to live. I stay at the cremation ground".

To this Swamiji remarked :- "I do not mind. I am neither afraid of the cremation ground nor do I get polluted by being there."

On the way, Bapumai went to the Chandrabhaga and threw the money into her waters, saying: "Mother, keep this with you." Then they went to the cremation ground. Bapumai enquired if Narasimha Swamiji was hungry. Swamiji said he was. In the meantime, a person dressed like a chef in a star hotel brought a plateful of dal, rice, chappatis and sweets. Bapumai asked Narasimha Swamiji to eat. Since he was hungry he sat down and ate all the food from the plate.

Narasimha Swamiji had a sumptuous meal. The attendant who brought food collected the empty plate and left the place. Swamiji wondered how the man came to that lonely place with such tasty food! But he dare not ask any questions in the presence of Bapumai.

Bapumai asked Swamiji, "So are you satisfied? What else do you want?"

Swamiji replied: "I want to see God."

Bapumai had a hearty laugh. She said: "You are a fool. Just now Lord Vithoba brought you the food. You could not recognise him. Except for the Lord Vithoba, who else can arrange for food at this lonely place?"

Narasimha Swamiji felt sorry that he could not recognise God in human form. Bapumai consoled him: "You are not yet ripe to see God who is omnipotent, omnipresent and omniscient. Your Guru is waiting in the North. He will guide you suitably."

As Narasimha Swamiji was about to take leave, Bapumai gave him a parting advice: "Except Lord Vittal there is nothing in the world. He is everywhere. He is in the front. He is at the back. He is above. He is below. You are Vittal and I am also Vittal. I have nothing more to say than this. Always keep this in mind, reflect on it, meditate on it and realize it. Now go northwards to meet your Guru."

So after a stint of twenty months, Narasimha Swamiji left Pandarapur in the beginning of 1932.

From 1932 to March 1934

＊A keen lover of poetry, Narasimha Swamiji memorized verses from the immortal works of poet-saints of Maharashtra, like Jnaneshwar, Namdev, Eknath, Tukaram and Samarth Ramdas. He moved extensively around Konkan, Pune and Nasik Districts and learnt by heart the philosophical poems of great saints of the region, like Mansur Mastana, Nipat Niranjan, Amrita Rai, Janardan Swami, Manpuri and others.

During all his wanderings he travelled mostly on foot and acquired wide experience of the world at large. He took mental notes of whatever he saw, and acquired knowledge of all the things that came his way. Thus when he got an opportunity he learnt Yogic postures and developed a strong and healthy body. Similarly, he gained detailed knowledge of Ayurveda and medicinal herbs and treated many an ailing person. He also learnt the intricacies of culinary art.

The difficulties Narasimha Swamiji had to face in his quest were many and varied. He used to walk along railway lines and sleep under bridges at night. He would never ask anyone for food or shelter and at times he had to go without food. He would only accept whatever was offered to him. Once, being oppressed by hunger, he softened mud with water, filtered it through a piece of cloth and ate it.

Narasimha Swamiji passed severe winter nights with only a towel round his waist. At night he would go to a tomb in the burial ground nearby, cover himself with the sheet spread on the tomb and replace it in the morning. Swamiji has thus lived in the open, has drunk water from flowing rivers, and has braved biting cold, oppressive heat and pouring rain with his almost naked body. As a result he suffered from malaria and chronic dysentery.

Narasimha Swamiji came in contact with a variety of men, from saints to rogues, but learnt something useful from each of them. Mostly he took shelter either in monasteries or temples. There, too, he had both good and bad experiences. On one or two occasions, the police harassed him.

Despite the hardships and trials that he had chosen to undergo, his restlessness of spirit remained so strong that he wandered all over Maharashtra. Many times he experienced the invisible hand of Providence guiding and protecting him. On one occasion, Swamiji was sitting at the Sholapur Railway Station. He had had no food for three days. A Sadhu came and sat near him. He ordered a plate of 'Puri-bhaji', out of which he gave only one 'puri' with a little 'bhaji' to Narasimha Swamiji. He gulped it, drank some water and fell asleep, saying to himself: "God has been kind, but rather thrifty." When he woke up, the Sadhu was still there. Immediately he gave the remaining plate of 'puri-bhaji', saying: "If one has fasted for three days, one should not eat too much all at once." Swamiji wondered how he knew that; but before he could ask him, the Sadhu vanished.

At Pune in the Cantonment area, he visited the dargah of famous Afghan saint Hazrat Baba Jan. He had heard about this woman saint and even though he developed a fascination for that place, Hazrat Baba Jan did not make any impact on him. At Vajreshwari, Swami Nityananda was quite popular by that time but was indifferent to Narasimha Swamiji. Swami Muktananda, an old companion of Narasimha Swamiji at Siddharudashram, Hubli, was staying in a *bhootkhana* near Chalisgaon and both of them took part in a *Nama-sankirthan* for a day.

The story of Narasimha Swamiji meeting Zipruanna – an *avadhooth* at Jalagaon is interesting. Narasimha Swamiji had heard that a great saint named Zipruanna and it is worth having his 'darshan'. Swamiji was disappointed to see him sitting on a heap of refuse, playing with the filth around him. He was surprised to see that though Zipruanna was sitting on a heap of refuse, his body was free from any trace of dust, dirt or repulsive odour. Instead, a pleasant fragrance emanated from his body. Swamiji was deeply fascinated by the saint's spiritual presence. When Narasimha Swamiji bowed down to him, Zipruanna curtly dismissed him saying: "I am not your Guru". In those days Narasimha Swamiji used to have severe headaches. He mentioned it to Zipruanna. The saint made Swamiji sit on his lap, licked his head and blessed him by saying: - "Your fame will reach the highest heaven". Swamiji was at once cured of his headaches.

Swamiji practised *tapasya* in a dense forest near the Vajreswari temple. Wild animals infested the place and there were occasions when tigers hovered round the place when he sat in meditation. Narasimha Swamiji chose to lead an austere life, to undergo privation and to remain in isolation. In his effort to keep as far away as possible from the din and bustle of life, he even passed days on hilltops, so that he could get nearer and nearer to the One he was seeking. Near Yeola, he lived with a Ramdasi sadhu to learn the Tulsi Ramayan – the Ram-charit-manas from him. He also looked after the cows owned by the sadhu.

Many a time Narasimha Swamiji lived only on buttermilk, milk or lemon juice for months together. Yet, with all the rigours of a wandering life, restlessness of spirit often got the better of him. He could hardly ever remain in one place for long. The indirect knowledge of God acquired through the scriptures did not satisfy him. He longed for direct contact. He was still in search of absolute reality. He did not mind which way he went – over the hills, down the dales, or by the riverside; through the dense forest or the plains – in fact anywhere, it hardly made any difference to him. He was in quest of God. He knew deep within his heart that the way could only be found from those who have already trodden the path and reached the goal. In other words, Narasimha Swamiji was in search of a Guru. Wherever he went he was anxious to know of saints and would go to them. He saw and met many sadhus, *tapasvins* in caves and *siddhas* sitting on garbage heaps. But he found none who would waken his soul to the tune of the Infinite. Or rather, none of them was acceptable to his buoyant spirit. He was like a fish eternally thirsty, or a bird always wanting to soar higher and still higher over the mountains, clouds and skies, to reach that supreme state of ever-conscious and all-pervading spirit. He wanted to become one with Him.

In the beginning of 1933, Narasimha Swamiji reached Khedgaon, which is close to Ahmednagar on the National Highway connecting Pune and Ahmednagar. At Khedgaon, Sadguru Bet Narayana Maharaj was living in an ashram. Narayana Maharaj was reputed to have been favoured with the grace of Lord Dattatreya in his infancy – as evidenced by the miracles he had wrought even as a boy of seven or eight. Narasimha Swamiji hoped to get guidance from Bet Narayana Maharaj.

The power of the Datta shrine, which was established by Narayana Maharaj was widely publicized. As Narasimha Swamiji sat in the temple, it occurred to him to put to test both Lord Dattatreya and his *upasaka*, Sadguru Bet Narayana Maharaj.

Narasimha Swamiji saw a number of sparrows chirping and flying about in the temple hall. He said to himself that if Lord Dattatreya and his *upasaka* were really possessed of superhuman spiritual powers attributed to them, one of the sparrows should sit on Narasimha Swamiji's head.

With this thought he closed his eyes and sat in meditation. Within five minutes, Narasimha Swamiji felt something strike his head. When he opened his eyes, he saw a sparrow flying away from him, after touching his head with its wing. No sparrow had touched Narasimhas Swamiji before this. This compliance with his request for proof filled Narasimha Swamiji with the conviction that Lord Dattatreya installed in the shrine and Sadguru Bet Narayana Maharaj were really possessed of superhuman spiritual powers.

As the only thing Narasimha Swamiji wanted was a divine personality, a perfect saint, whom he could contact and who could control him in circumstances favouring perfect surrender, Swamiji approached Sadguru Bet Narayana Maharaj and asked him for this favour. Since he had to make his request in the presence of many people, Narasimha Swamiji clothed his request in symbolic and figurative speech.

Narasimha Swamiji said : "I am a merchant dealing in gems, but I am a very unfortunate dealer. I have come across many gems, but none of them has satisfied me so far. Each gem, I get is very tiny and has dots, cracks or other flaws. Will you please bless me so that I may get one pure, big, flawless diamond?"

Sadguru Bet Narayana Maharaj, after a moment's thought, replied, "Yes, you will have your desire fulfilled". This was in the beginning of 1933. It however, took sometime for Narasimha Swamiji to get the promised invaluable diamond.

Narasimha Swamiji stayed in the quiet serene atmosphere of the Datta shrine in Khedgaon for sometime. Later Bet Narayana Maharaj came down to Bangalore in September 1945 and performed *homes* for five long days. The very next day that is on 3rd September 1945, he attained 'Mahasamadhi'. His devotees have erected a suitable Samadhi shrine for Bet Narayana Maharaj at a place next to Sri Gavi Gangadhareswara temple in Gavipuram Extension of Bangalore.

Even when he was at Khedgaon, Narasimha Swamiji learnt about Avatar Meher Baba, a Parsi saint who was living in Meherbad, 5 km north of Ahmednagar. Meher Baba was much talked of as a perfect master who had toured round the world. Meher Baba was born in Pune in 1894 and was initiated into the spiritual path by Hazrat Baba Jan. He spread the message of universal love. After taking leave from Sadguru Bet Narayana Maharaj, Narasimha Swamiji reached Meherbad by the end of 1933.

Just twenty days prior to Narasimha Swamiji reaching Meherbad, Avatar Meher Baba had taken a vow of life-long silence.

He communicated with devotees through the help of a slate. When Narasimha Swamiji sought spiritual guidance, Avatar Meher Baba wrote in Devanagari script on the slate – "I am not your Guru. Your Guru is waiting for you in the North." Meher Baba maintained the vow of silence till his Mahasamadhi in January 1969.

Although disappointed at first, Narasimha Swamiji stayed for sometime in Meherbad. He made an indepth study of the life and teachings of Avatar Meher Baba. He also met several devotees directed by Upasini Maharaj of Sakori to meet Avatar Meher Baba. From them he learnt the greatness of Upasini Maharaj and also was guided to reach Sakori.

At Sakori

Narasimha Swamiji's meeting Upasini Maharaj and his life at the Sakori Ashram formed an important landmark in his spiritual pursuit.

Sakori is a small village, close to Chithali on the Ahmednagar-Kopergaon railway line, 80 km away from Ahmednagar. Narasimha Swamiji reached Upasini Maharaj's ashram on a fine evening in March 1934. The ashram is adjacent to a burial ground. Upasini Maharaj was conversing with a few of his followers. Upasini Maharaj had a clairvoyant vision and the moment Narasimha Swamiji arrived, he welcomed him saying: - "At last you have come. I have been waiting for you for quite sometime." Narasimha Swamiji at that moment did not know the significance of Upasini Maharaj expecting his arrival.

Upasini Maharaj had undergone his spiritual pursuit under Sai Baba's guidance and was a realized soul. Sai Baba had in fact groomed him to be his successor. Unfortunately Sai Baba had strictly asked him to practise spiritual 'sadhana' for four years. Upasini Maharaj followed his instructions for three years and ten months and ran away from Shirdi two months before he could complete the rigorous training. Therefore, he had missed the golden opportunity of becoming an heir to Sai Baba. Nevertheless he had evolved into being a great saint.

Upasini Baba's reputation was so great that Mahatma Gandhi had approached him in 1927 with a view to securing his blessings for national welfare. Inspite of his greatness, Upasini Baba was in deep crisis at that time and to help him come out of this situation, Providence had made Narasimha Swamiji reach Sakori at the opportune moment.

The exact position was this. In the days of yore, women in Hindu religion had equal rights as men for chanting the Vedas and performing Yagnas. Later on, the Hindu fanatics denied this privilege to women. In order to restore these rights to women, Upasini Maharaj undertook a revolutionary step. In order to permit Vedic chanting and perform Yagnas, he married 65 virgin girls by holding an idol of Lord Krishna. While Upasini Maharaj was past sixty years of age, all the girls were under twenty-five years of age. It was indeed a rare and an extraordinary event. Even though it was well intentioned, a good majority of the devotees of Upasini Maharaj considered it as a heinous crime and filed a public interest litigation in the courts of Nagpur and Mumbai. The courts also had taken the subject seriously and had issued summons to Upasini Maharaj to appear before the court. It was feared that any moment Upasini Maharaj could be arrested on charges of practising polygamy.

Upasini Maharaj was searching for a suitable advocate to plead on his behalf in the court of law. Not a single advocate in Maharashtra was prepared to take up his case, as no one endorsed Upasini Baba's action. There was a public outcry against Upasini Maharaj. Upasini Baba's ashram, which used to attract thousands of devotees, had become virtually empty.

Upasini Baba's welcome word to Narasimha Swamiji - 'I am waiting for you' meant that Narasimha Swamiji who had given up his legal profession should again wear the Lawyer's robes and plead for him at Nagpur and Mumbai courts of Law. Narasimha Swamiji, who had given up his legal practice in 1925 to become a mendicant, was at first reluctant to again become an advocate. Ultimately he agreed to Upasini Maharaj's request and prepared himself for a prolonged legal battle.

This litigation went on for thirty months. He had to travel to Mumbai, Nagpur, Ajmer and other places to examine witnesses. There were 265 witnesses. Ultimately, both at Nagpur and Mumbai, the courts dismissed the petitions after acquitting Upasini Maharaj as 'not guilty'.

While attending to the litigation work of Upasini Maharaj at Mumbai and Nagpur, Narasimha Swamiji had a dose of pilgrimage too. Having heard about Saint Tajuddin Baba as a perfect Master, he visited his samadhi shrine at Nagpur. Similarly, he undertook a pilgrimage to the Khwaja Moinuddin Chisty Dargah Sharif at Ajmer. At Pushkar in Rajastan, he paid his obeisance to Lord Brahma seeking His intervention in his quest for a Sadguru. He had a providential escape from the jaws of a crocodile while bathing at Pushkar Tirth. A timely shot from the rifle of a Sardarjee killed the crocodile and Narasimha Swamiji's life was saved. The wound inflicted was quite grave and Narasimha Swamiji's right leg was in bandage for months together and even after the wound healed, he limped for years!

In these thirty months, Narasimha Swamiji had delved deep into the life and mission of Upasini Maharaj. He evinced a keen interest in his teachings. He collected from the Master whatever information he could about his life and pieced them together in a systematic and chronological order. With the help of Sri Kakade and Sri Chitnis – two intimate devotees of Upasini Maharaj, he compiled Upasini Baba's life and teachings and published a book 'The Sage of Sakori' in August 1936. This publication is interesting to devotees of Upasini Maharaj as also to those of Sai Baba as it presents valuable information on how Sai Baba had trained a spiritual aspirant in self purification, developing 'Ekagrachitta' (single-mindedness), devotion and implicit obedience to the Guru and seeing God in every living creature. The teachings of Upasini Baba incorporated in this book are of practical value to aspirants. 'The Sage of Sakori' is, as 'Self Realization' the first authentic biography of Upasini Maharaj in English. Through this book, he introduced the greatness of Upasini Maharaj to the external world.

How much chastening Narasimha Swamiji had undergone in the hard life he had lived in all these years, following the catastrophe in his domestic life, and what spiritual progress he had made by now may be assessed in the following passage taken from page 63 of 'The Sage of Sakori'. While discussing Narasimha Swamiji's bereavements, the following questions were mooted. "Why should this happen to him? What is the meaning of life?" The following passage contains the answer.

"God declares that in giving His grace to a devotee, He deprives him of every possession and all attractions as these hold down the soul to the earth, and prevent the upward gaze which dwells upon and absorbs or is absorbed in Him."

Upasini Maharaj advised Narasimha Swamiji to stick to the 'Bhakti marga' and not to fritter away his powers in metaphysical speculation. He also asked Narasimha Swamiji to develop his knowledge and tendencies through well recognised methods such as Japa, Bhajan, Pranayama etc., He also enjoined on him the life of an 'Akinchana', a holy ascetic.

While practising his 'sadhana' in accordance with Upasini Maharaj's advice, Narasimha Swamiji was startled to discover that there were elements in Upasini Maharaj's teachings and methods which jarred on him and which went very much against the opinions and expectations which Narasimha Swamiji held about correct religious life. So Narasimha Swamiji decided to leave Upasini Maharaj's ashram towards the end of August, 1936.

By now Narasimha Swamiji may be said to have arrived at the very end of his search. He was like a lost child seeking his parents going from one teacher to another. Meanwhile, he was also qualifying himself for a higher work awaiting him, the mission for which he was born.

Shirdi is not far from Sakori. Narasimha Swamiji had heard about Shirdi from Upasini Maharaj and wrote down in the publication 'The Sage of Sakori' how much Sai Baba had helped Upasini Maharaj. He had set apart in that work, a chapter from

pages 38 to 41 to give a brief account of Sai Baba. Still it did not
occur to him to pay a visit to Sai Baba's samadhi at Shirdi till the
destined hour had arrived. Since Sai Baba had already taken up
'Mahasamadhi' in 1918, Narasimha Swamiji thought it was not
worthwhile to visit Shirdi. Further, even Upasini Maharaj too did
not motivate him to visit Shirdi. It is very true that 'everything
happens according to His will and His time.'

Part-III

God Realization

Face to face with the Master

—◦—

It was 29th August 1936, Sravan Poornima – the holy Upakarma day. Also 'Rakhi Poornima' when sisters wish their brothers all the best in life. Generally Brahmins changed over to a new set of sacred thread, after discarding the old one. It is celebrated all over the country as a festival, with sumptuous food and rejoicing in life. Narasimha Swamiji got up at 4 am and was in a pensive mood. He contemplated his good old days with his family members at Salem. In these eleven years of itinerant life, he could neither get a Guru to guide him nor did his confused mind become still. He was disappointed and dejected in life. He made up his mind to leave Upasini Baba's ashram once and for all and get back to Madras to spend the rest of his life with his eldest son Venkataraman and his family. He was firmly convinced that he was not destined to get peace of mind in this birth.

Narasimha Swamiji was afraid that Upasini might influence him to reverse the decision if he conveyed his intention to get back to Madras. So from a distance, he bowed down to Upasini Maharaj and mentally sought his permission to leave.

Narasimha Swamiji came out of the ashram and as he was crossing the cremation ground, a six-foot tall, well-built man of Pathan origin accosted him and questioned him: - "Oh Madrasi Sadhu! Where are you going?" Swamiji answered him: - "I had an itinerant life for a few years in spiritual pursuit. Now I am going back to my native place." The Pathan pleaded: - "Anyway you are going back. Before you leave, have 'darshan' of Sai Baba's 'samadhi' at Shirdi. Maybe, you could be benefited spiritually". Narasimha Swamiji was getting bored with this conversation and hence curtly replied – "Sai Baba has attained 'Mahasamadhi' eighteen years ago in 1918. A darshan of his samadhi will not benefit me in any manner. I have already visited dargahs of Hazrat Baba Jan, Tajuddin Baba, and Khwaja Moinuddin Chisty Sheriff. None of them has made any impact on me."

The Pathan was not prepared to accept defeat so easily. He virtually pleaded: - "Go over to Shirdi once. Sai Baba is ever living and active. He will certainly help you in your spiritual upliftment". Narasimha Swamiji was looking forward to escape from this adamant Pathan. He simply said 'yes' and left the place.

Narasimha Swamiji's earlier plan was to walk up to Chitali Railway Station and from there to catch a train to get back to Madras. But the persistent request of the Pathan made him change his route and unknowingly his feet led him to Shirdi – seven kilometers away from Sakori.

When Narasimha Swamiji reached Shirdi, it was already 11 am in the forenoon. Abdulla Baba was fanning Sai Baba's samadhi with peacock feathers.

Narasimha Swamiji visiting the samadhi of Sai Baba is a memorable event in his life and it also opened a new chapter in the spiritual regeneration of so many of us. He stood silently watching the samadhi. It was the happiest moment in his life. For eighteen years Sai Baba was keeping his treasure, all the while eagerly waiting for a suitable recipient for his grace and bounty. Sai Baba like a magnificent wave of fire engulfed each and every one of the millions of cells in Narasimha Swamiji's body and in lieu thereof granted him a new life. The old body of Narasimha Swamiji was no more and it became Sai-Swaroopi Narasimha Swamiji. Everything happened in a flash of a split second. Narasimha Swamiji became a realized soul then and there and within no time had become a part and parcel of Sai Baba. In other words Narasimha Swamiji has now retransformed into Sai Baba himself. Narasimha Swamiji's mind, which was in utter confusion, became totally still. His mind was clear as the blue sky. He became the receptacle of Sai's total bounty. Sai Baba kindled the light of enlightenment in Swamiji.

Narasimha Swamiji gained something from Ramana Bhagawan at Tiruvannamalai. He shared his gains with us by publishing *Self-Realization – Biography of Ramana Maharishi*. He came in for some more gains at Sakori and he gave us 'The Sage of Sakori'. At Shirdi he profited to his maximum capacity and the world is receiving high dividends from Narasimha Swamiji even at this moment.

Swamiji said, in October 1941 at a group meeting in Kolkata – "My hunger for spiritual food was not satisfied till I came over to Shirdi. At Shirdi I was given more than I could take. I had at last discovered my Sadguru. He Samartha Sadguru Sainath Maharaj and I live in constant communion with Him".

Early days of Sai Prachar

Narasimha Swamiji did not want to leave Shirdi after he gained Self-Realization. He has stated in one place "At last I have come to my Gurudeva. I obtained my Sadguru. Words fail me to describe his greatness and the abundant spiritual power he possesses. He has given me unbound confidence and has made me perfect in everything. He is Love incarnate. He fulfills all my desires."

Narasimha Swamiji was surprised to find how for nearly sixty years a great one had lived and blessed so many in this neglected village and a few from outside and only a few had know him and among them too how little of him they knew. Swamiji was determined to take Sai Baba out from here and make him known first in Maharashtra. He would carry Baba's message to his home province, touring every town and hamlet and then spread the gospel everywhere in India.

Shirdi Samsthan was impressed with the piety and zeal shown by a southerner. The daily pooja begun when Sai Baba was in the flesh was continued at his samadhi. Narasimha Swamiji suggested a few modifications to make it as per the traditional method of worship. He also composed 'Sai Ashtotharam', in which he poured out his devotion and wisdom. This has been incorporated in the daily service going on at the Samadhi Mandir in Shirdi. Herein may be found evidence of Sai Baba's acceptance of the devotion of Narasimha Swamiji.

Before embarking on his enterprise, Narasimha Swamiji had to find out more about Sai Baba. He knew enough Marathi to enquire and collect information about Sai Baba from those who were lucky enough to come into personal contact with the Master. In Shirdi itself Abdullah Baba was still living. He had swept the street, watered the Lendi Garden and filled water tubs for his Master in Dwarakamayi. There was Ganapathy Rao Dattatreya Sahasrabudhe, a former Police Head Constable, who was delivering 'Harikathas' and discourses on Sai Maharaj. He was Sai Baba's favourite and was called Das Ganu Maharaj. Das Ganu Maharaj extended his wholehearted co-operation. There was Justice Sri M.B.Rege of Indore and many others who had met Sai Baba and were blessed by him.

By 1936, Narasimha Swamiji was sixty-two years old. He was suffering from rheumatoid arthritis, an ailment affecting the body joints and virtually immobilizing him on all cold winter days. But Swamiji, whom Sai Baba had given his entire spiritual treasure was full of enthusiasm and vigorously took up his new project of taking Sai Baba to the masses.

His first assignment in this direction was to record the experiences of those devotees who had personal contact with Sai Baba. Narasimha Swamiji went round, made enquiries and recorded their statements. These statements show how miraculously Sai Baba had helped his devotees rescuing them from dangers, granting their prayers and messages etc. He found them all interesting and wonderful. He felt how important it was to publicize Sai Baba throughout our vast country. He therefore compiled these statements for publication. These statements were long afterwards published in three parts in English and Tamil, under the title *Devotees' Experiences*.

While engaged in this labour of love, Narasimha Swamiji discovered that Sai Baba was really Lord Ramachandra or Lord Krishna who had been born in the modern world for the welfare of mankind, that his power for good was as potent even after his death as it had been when he was alive, and he was worthy of worship as God-incarnate. Narasimha Swamiji found in Sai Baba the 'Trinity' and took upon himself the mission of propagating the Sai-faith.

Narasimha Swamiji looked for a biography if any, about Sai Baba. Das Ganu Maharaj had already composed 'Sri Sai Leelamrit' in Marathi. Rao Bahadur M.V.Pradhan, a solicitor of Santa Cruz, who had met Sai Baba had written a small book in English entitled 'Glimpses of Spirituality'. An authoritative work, which had received the approval and blessing of Sai Baba, was 'Shri Sai Satcharitra' in verses in Marathi by Anna Sahib Dhabolkar who was nicknamed 'Hemadpant' by the Master.

Narasimha Swamiji added to all that he had heard and recorded as statements, by reading the literature mentioned above. His discovery of a Sadguru may be said to be complete by now. Then with Justice Sri M.B.Rege and Das Ganu Maharaj, he toured Maharashtra extensively addressing mass meetings in English and Marathi. Meanwhile, he published a series of articles on Sai Baba in the 'Sunday Times' of Madras.

All these activities occupied Narasimha Swamiji till the end of 1938 and in the beginning of 1939 he returned to Madras.

Baba himself favours the movement

The task of collecting facts about Sai Baba was by no means easy. While not much information was readily available, it was difficult to find unbiased sources of information,

As a rule, as Narasimha Swamiji writes on page 97 of his book 'The Sage of Sakori', devotees are not the best observers of the powers and doings of their Gurus, from the chronicler's viewpoint. "Their crudity, love of exaggeration, over-sensitiveness in trying to avoid anything like strict examination of seeming miracles and mysteries, and usual want of the scientific attitude of training account for the unreliability of their testimony."

After statements had been obtained from devotees and others, there arose the further difficulty of removing the grain from the chaff, or sifting and arranging all the mass of evidence collected, and of presenting what, after enquiry and investigations, could be accepted as true and beyond reasonable doubt.

Those who have read Narasimha Swamiji's biographies of Ramana Maharishi, Upasini Maharaj and Sai Baba and his accounts of the numerous devotees of Sai Baba can only marvel at the amount of trouble Narasimha Swamiji must have taken in collecting and processing the information and producing the final narration strictly in accordance with the norms of scientific and objective inquiry.

Only one blessed with Divine grace could have summoned to his aid the enormous patience, perseverance and faith without which the task undertaken would not have become an accomplished fact.

Narasimha Swamiji himself has narrated as follows:-

"For collecting experience of devotees who were directly blessed by Sai Baba, I received many invitations. On one such assignment I went to Pune and was introduced to the Rasanes. As I was taking down notes of their experiences, Sri Narayan Purushotham Avasthi, son of Justice Sri P.R.Avasthi of Gwalior, came in and took me to his father, who was a great devotee of Sai Baba.

"The moment he learnt of my mission, Justice Sri P.R.Avasthi, the sincere soul that he is, was overjoyed and, treated me as he would treat an old and dear friend, he placed himself and his influence entirely at my disposal. He introduced me to about sixty devotees of Sai Baba who had personal experiences of Sai Baba's greatness.

"Most of these devotees were ignorant of English and could speak only in Marathi, which was unfamiliar to me at the time. Justice Sri Avasthi's knowledge of Marathi and English was of great service to me as his influence and zeal to serve the cause of devotion to Baba in collecting, editing and publishing information about Baba.

"From the very beginning, I was determined to collect, test and sift such materials, to arrange them on their strength, that is, on their inherent reliability and credibility, and compile a biography of Baba that would benefit earnest souls all over India if not also beyond.

"For many months I was engaged in this work with the invaluable help of Justice Sri Avasthi who interpreted to me Hemadpant's 'Sri Sai Satcharita, Sri Sai Lila Masik and other Marathi publications on Sai Baba. He was a great help to me in this way for one year or so vigorously that at the end of that period, I found that I could read and translate the Marathi book myself without his help, with occasional reference to a dictionary.

"This itself was proof of Sai Baba's grace flowing towards me. But fresh evidence of his grace became manifest off and on in the course of this work.

"Spiritual experiences, especially the sadhaka's experiences with his Guru or with God, are so intensely personal and unique to him, touch such inner depths of his soul, and are so intimate that they (the spiritual experiences) are not to be communicated to anybody, much less to strangers. But, as it happened, barring a few, everyone of Baba's devotees whom we approached was very soon impelled to unlock the portals of his heart and let us into his secret experiences.

"A Public Prosecutor, who was an intimate friend of Justice Sri Avasthi, began, within a few minutes of his introduction to me, to unburden himself and relate his innermost experiences disclosing facts which he had not till then revealed even to his best friend, Justice Sri Avasthi.

"I typed out these statements and left the bunch of papers with my friend, Sri G.B.Datar, an advocate at Thane. When I was at Pune, Sri Datar intimated to me that the bunch of papers I had left with him was lost and could not be found inspite of his best efforts.

"As I had no copies of these statements, their loss would prove a very serious handicap to the progress of my work. Full of faith in Sai Baba and praying to him for their recovery, I immediately went to Thane. On reaching Sri Datar's house, I went to his table on which I had placed the papers. In a minute or two, I placed my hand on a bundle among his legal papers and this turned out to be the missing bunch.

"More than one devotee warned me against accepting bogus devotees and faked experiences and asked me how I, a stranger to men, manners and language of Maharashtra, hoped to ensure the purity and reliability of the information I received. I knew one and only device. Sai Baba was my guide and he would not allow humbug to pass into my sacred collection.

"At least in two cases I received strange and unexpected warnings and revelations indicating what I should reject. Some statements were thus wholly rejected and some in part. It was quite obvious to me as also to my Mumbai friends, that Sai Baba was favouring the publication, by me, of his biography and was removing the obstacles thereto, step by step.

"After collecting about 15 statements, I began publishing parts of them in English in the columns of the *Sunday Times* – Madras. In 1937 this account appeared in 30 or 40 issues of that journal. As the journal had a circulation of 20,000, the initial work of creating among the devout public all over India an interest in Sai Baba got off to a very good start.

"This publicity had a further good result. A highly placed friend remarked to me that these experiences, by themselves, produced a very unfavourable impression, because they made Baba look like some sort of a juggler with rare powers rather than a great soul.

"When I replied, 'What about Sri Krishna's miracles?' he said, 'Oh, but they are part of Sri Krishna's nature.' 'Exactly,' I retorted ' so are the miracles of Baba are part of Baba's nature'. 'That is what is left out of your articles,' my friend pointed out.

"My friend was right. He is a pure and holy person, not afflicted with jealousy or hatred of saints other than his own Guru. He represents a group that, in its desire to stress metaphysical and ultimate truths, is apt to underrate the importance of miracles to those who are just beginning their spiritual life.

"So I felt that the entire defect was that I was producing the separate bricks lent to me by each devotee in the shape of his experience. Hardly any of these devotees had a conception of what the edifice was into which his brick had to be fitted. Hardly any of them knew the real nature of Baba. So I appealed to Baba himself much as Sri Ramakrishna complained to Kali Matha that a learned pandit should represent her as a 'tamasic' deity.

"I felt an inner warning that I should abandon thinking in English and in terms of newspaper articles and that I should try to write out a reliable but orthodox biography of the saint in my own mother tongue.

"As I began that task, even in the earliest chapters, Baba's nature, his powers, their nature, his Guru and what his Guru did for him all these came up for consideration.

"And I discovered passages in Baba's sayings (utterances, discourses) which, read with passages from the scriptures, showed how Baba's Guru was saturated with divinity, how indeed, that Guru was God himself, how that Guru-God's self was poured (superimposed) upon Baba leading to Baba's merger in the Divine and the consequent manifestation of miraculous powers.

"What Baba was taught and what Baba taught or conveyed by means of radiation or unseen influence came to me in flashes to fill up the picture of Baba, which I was trying to draw.

"For the first time, so far as I knew, a clearly intelligible picture of Baba's nature, his powers and the course of his life materialized and were presented by me in 'Introduction to Sai Baba.' The first edition of this was published in November 1939 and, within eleven months, a third edition was published and rapidly circulated.

"The experiences of the devotees as narrated by them have also been published as parts I and II in support of much that is contained in the *Introduction to Sai Baba*. This was later rendered into all the languages of the south – Tamil, Malayalam, Kannada and Telugu. These facts are clear evidence that Sai Baba was in favour of the spread of the Sai Bhakti movement.

"One striking fact supporting the above conclusion is that thousands upon thousands of people became devotees of Baba in the South within the space of a few months. Meetings were held where 'arathis' were conducted and a few words about Sai Baba were said.

"Baba's support of the movement can be seen also by the fact that many people from all parts of the country who became his devotees have had several experiences of their own which they communicated to me. These have been published under the title "Devotees' Experiences."

The only aim

———◆———

Narasimha Swamiji attained Self-Realization on 29th August, 1936, and in right earnest set out to distribute the benefits of Sai-Treasure that he obtained from Sai Baba. Shuddhananda Bharathi Swamiji was a contemporary of Narasimha Swamiji and also his companion first at the Ramana Ashram in Tiruvannamalai and later at the Upasini Baba Ashram in Sakori. On watching Narasimha Swamiji's peaceful and glowing face, Shuddhananda Bharathi Swamiji went into a dilemma.

Shuddhananda Bharathi Swamiji was staying with Sai Baba for sometime at Shirdi. He was an inmate of Upasini Baba's ashram at Sakori. He also stayed for some time at the Ramakrishna Mutt at Kolkata with direct disciples of Ramakrishna and Swami Vivekananda. He made pilgrimages to Badri, Kedar, Rishikesh, Haridwar, Kashi etc. He was well versed not only in Ramayana, Mahabharata, and Bhagawatham but also in Koran and Bible. He was in spiritual quest much earlier than Narasimha Swamiji.

Inspite of all these prerequisites and other qualifications he had a wandering mind and did not have the stillness of mind. He was far from the goal of Self-Realization. Intimate contact with realized souls like Sai Baba, Ramana, Upasini Maharaj had not brought him peace of mind.

He made a submission to Upasini Maharaj about his disappointment. He expressed his happiness at Narasimha Swamiji's realization through Sai Baba's grace. Upasini listened to him patiently and told him he would answer the question later in the same night. Incidentally he invited Suddhananda Bharathi Swamiji to attend a dinner at Upasini Baba's Ashram that night.

Elaborate arrangements were made for the dinner. Many dishes – sweets and savouries were prepared. At the right time Suddhananda Bharathi Swamiji arrived at Upasini Baba's ashram. He was the only guest and was honourably well received. He was served several varieties of food items. Upasini Maharaj did not join him for dinner but made him eat different sweets and food items. Pleased by the generosity of the host, Suddhananda Bharathi Swamiji ate to his heart's content and in fact over and above what his stomach could take in. At the end of the dinner, it was even difficult for him to get up. Virtually he had to be lifted and carried to the rest room.

It was a restless night for Suddhananda Bharathi Swamiji. He developed severe pain in his abdomen. He had continuous diarrhoea. He had not a single wink of sleep. He spent the entire night in agony. As the next morning dawned, he was vexed with life.

In the morning Upasini Maharaj enquired of Suddhananda Bharathi Swamiji as to whether he had restful sleep. Suddhananda Bharathi Swamiji had no strength even to answer this question. "What rest could I take? In the entire night I suffered with agonizing pain in abdomen and repeatedly going to the toilet. I am even unable to stand now."

Suddhananda Bharathi complained to Upasini Maharaj that he was yet to get a reply for his question as to why he had not got realization inspite of his scholarship and intimate contact with great saints. Upasini Maharaj laughed over it and answered him: - "Your present condition answers your query. You have sufficient scholarship and wisdom. But you do not have the one pointed goal. You are only accumulating knowledge but you don't know what exactly you want to achieve by these pursuits. Yours is more a diarrhoea of knowledge. Hence you are yet to get realization.

Narasimha Swamiji's one and only goal was to secure a Sadguru who could guide him to Self-Realization. All his efforts were in this one pointed direction. After eleven years of Herculean efforts for his one-pointed goal, Sai Baba blessed him with Self-Realization."

This revelation of Upasini Maharaj about Narsimha Swamiji's efforts 'in quest of a Sadguru' is a beacon for all Sai devotees.

With a repulsive leper

———◆———

After realizing Sai Baba, Narasimha Swamiji had another thrilling experience at Sakori. One day, maybe in the month of November or December 1936, Upasini Maharaj held an open feast. There were many invitees including Swami Ram Baba who lived in the company of Sai Baba for a long time.

As the feast was about to end, an old man suffering from leprosy came along. The leper had a frightening appearance. He had only one eye; blood and pus were oozing from his disfigured lips, nose and eyes; he had open ulcers all over his body. As if this were not enough, an awful stench also emanated from his body. Everyone was aghast at this sight.

Imagine Swami Ram Baba's bewilderment when Upasini Baba told him: "Feed the old man with your own hands. He is not able to eat by himself." Swami Ram Baba pulled himself together as best as he could and started feeding the repulsive leper. He however took great care to see that his hand did not touch the bleeding lips of the leper. As a result, some of the food kept dropping down.

After the leper had eaten and walked away, Upasini Maharaj said to Swami Ram Baba: "Pick up the food from the plate and eat it." To eat the food that had been contaminated by the bleeding lips of the leper seemed impossible to Swami Ram Baba. Despite a desperate effort, he could eat only one morsel.

At this, Upasini Maharaj looked at Narasimha Swamiji. Without any hesitation, Narasimha Swamiji took the plate from

Swami Ram Baba and ate up all the remnants without the least hesitation. As everybody looked on in amazement, Upasini told the assembled devotees: "Did you see how swiftly the old man walked away? Is it possible for one so terribly afflicted by open sores and leprosy to walk like that? Do you know who came here in the garb of a repulsive leper? It was none other than Shirdi Sai Baba himself. Only Narasimha Swamiji who sees Sai Baba in every body could identify him." Narasimha Swamiji realized with great joy that Lord Sainath himself had come to instruct him not to attach importance to the external superficialities of existence but to realize that Lord Sainath and Lord Sainath alone pervades everything and every being.

This incident has played a very significant part in shaping Narasimha Swamiji's outlook and approach to life, placing him on a firm spiritual foundation. The invisible hand of Lord Sainath was guiding him in every moment of his life and Narasimha Swamiji's surrender to Sai Baba was total.

Part-IV

Narasimha Swamiji's Mission

Early days of his Mission

Narasimha Swamiji searched for his Sadguru, discovered him and then shared with us all the grace he received from his Sadguru. This is briefly the story of his life.

Avatar Meher Baba knew best the value and the esoteric aspect of Sai Baba and four other perfect Masters working with him. The five perfect Masters of our age, according to Meher Baba are: Sai Baba, Upasini Maharaj, Hazrat Baba Jan, Tajuddin Baba and Bet Narayana Maharaj. Among these Sai Baba holds the highest place – Sai Baba is, along with the other perfect Masters even now directing the force of the Universe in the different spheres of life. Prof. C.G.Narke mentioned in his statement to Narasimha Swamiji that Sai Baba seemed to be working not only among us but also in other worlds unseen and unknown to us.

So powerful is Sai Baba that no man could go to him unless he was called. Sai Baba called Narasimha Swamiji and Swamiji responded to the call. Other devotees have written about Sai Baba's life and had sung his glories before and after the advent of Narasimha Swamiji, but none could do so much and accomplish so well, because Sai Baba willed it and has chosen Narasimha Swamiji as an efficient instrument to work for him.

Narasimha Swamiji returned to Madras in 1939 and his sole aim was to spread the Sai movement all over the country. During 1936 to 1939, he had already travelled all over Maharashtra on lecture tours along with Das Ganu Maharaj, Justice Sri M.B.Rege and Justice Sri P.R.Avasthi and had created a sensation among the public. Sai Baba's name which was confined only to Shirdi and a few neighbouring villages earlier had now become a household word in Maharashtra. Thousands of people from nooks and corners of Maharashtra had already started visiting Shirdi. Narasimha Swamiji desired to take Sai Baba's name all over India.

Narasimha Swamiji found that Shirdi Samsthan of Sri Sai Baba had a 'Bhakta Mandal' (an association of Sai devotees) of which Sai devotees could become a member. But the Bhakta Mandal had no branch anywhere and it did not mean to open any. The only activity of the Bhakta Mandal was to send 'udhi prasad' three times in a year. Narasimha Swamiji therefore felt the need for forming an All India Sai Samaj with the object of disseminating the Sai movement in our country. Accordingly, the first step he took, on returning to Madras in 1939 was to start the All India Sai Samaj with its office at Mylapore, Madras. The main objective of this Samaj was to create awareness among people about Sai Baba and lead them to spiritual glory.

Narasimha Swamiji was absorbed at all times in thinking of and talking about Sai Baba alone and nothing else. His constant communion with Sai Baba, his private talks at group meetings and public lectures fostered his influence, and attracted a band of volunteers around him.

Narasimha Swamiji's first publication 'Who is Sai Baba?' came out in 1939. Priced at an anna per copy it proved popular. By producing a Tamil edition, Swamiji reached a wider public. In 1940 came 'Wondrous Saint Sai Baba' priced at six annas a copy. In this book he has given more details and interestingly the author shows how in previous incarnations help rendered was general and in 'Sai incarnation' the Lord's grace was distributed individually and severally. Narasimha Swamiji also shows the steps by which Sai Baba helps in the evolution of devotees. 'Wondrous Saint' has since been translated into Telugu, Hindi, Bengali and Gujrathi.

Narasimha Swamiji's magna carta 'The Charters and Sayings' came out next with a foreword by Justice Sri M.B.Rege. It is an inspired work. It combines the boons granted by Sai Baba to his devotees with Baba's teachings and biography. It is made of short paragraphs under suitable headings. It is written in Biblical style. On account of the topical treatment followed by the author, the book may be opened at any page and read with pleasure. The index affords valuable assistance to volunteers in selecting topics on which to write or deliver public lectures. This has gone into several reprints and is now published as 'Gospel of Sai Baba' also in Tamil, Kannada, Telugu, Hindi and Malayalam.

How much this book has helped in the Sai movement may be seen from the following incident. 'Charters and Sayings' reached the reading public all over Madras Presidency including Mysore, Travancore and other native states. Papaiah Chetty, a rich Zamindar of Nellore, was very much influenced by this book. He met Narasimha Swamiji at Shirdi on 23ʳᵈ December 1940 and handed over to him a bundle containing Rs.11, 455/-. He just told him that Sai Baba had instructed him to give this to Narasimha Swamiji, who would get further instructions from Sai Baba about its usage and left. Narasimha Swamiji who had renounced property worth a million and become a mendicant hesitated for a minute. He composed himself and wrote on three slips to know Sai Baba's mind on using this fund: -

1. This amount to be used for Sai *prachar,*
2. This amount to be put in a fixed deposit and use the interest for a good cause,
3. Hand over this amount to the Trustees of Shirdi Samsthan towards the Temple corpus fund.

A child who came to the Samadhi Mandir was asked to pick up a slip. The baby picking up the slip at number one above saw Sai Baba's will. Narasimha Swamiji asked the Trustees of Shirdi Samsthan if they would keep the amount for using it on 'Sai Prachar' work. On their declining his offer Narasimha Swamiji brought the money to Madras.

In January 1940 he started a monthly magazine 'Sai Sudha' with Tamil, Sanskrit and Telugu sections added to the main English section. S.R.Sampathkumran was the first Editor till he passed away on 21ˢᵗ October 1943. Swami Sivananda and Sri Radhakrishna Swamiji edited the magazine in later years. Narasimha Swamiji published the "Devotees' Experiences" in three parts in English and Tamil.

By then the All India Sai Samaj was in dire need of an enthusiastic and young person to shoulder the executive responsibility of its activities. Narasimha Swamiji also needed a personal secretary to whom he could dictate text so that more books on Sai Baba could be brought out. Sai Baba in his inimitable manner fulfilled these two needs.

Sri O.K.Varada Rao, son-in-law of Justice Sri Somaiah of Madras High Court, was then an officer in the Bank of Baroda at Madras. This enthusiastic young man became the first Honorary Secretary of the All India Sai Samaj. His wife Smt.Sharada not only became an 'Ankitha Puthri' (foster daughter) to Narasimha Swamiji but also served him as his Personal Secretary in taking down all his dictations, prepare manuscript, typing them, correct spelling mistakes, send them to the press, correcting the proofs and bring out the final version. The 'Sharada touch' can be seen in all the publications of Narasimha Swamiji. Apart from this she used to plan Swamiji's travel programmes, lecture tours and other engagements.

Smt.Sharada expressed a doubt to Narasimha Swamiji when she and her husband first met him at the All India Sai Samaj. Swamiji was feeding sparrows at that time. Her doubt was, "When we accept Sai Baba as God, should we continue to worship other deities such as Lakshmi, Saraswathi, Ganesha etc., Sai Baba represents total Godhood while all other deities represent a specific function. So is it not enough if we worship only Sai Baba and none else?"

Narasimha Swamiji replied to her :- "Sharada, this body, which you are seeing, is named Narasimha Swamiji. This has several organs for various functions. Mouth is used to eat. Ears for hearing, eyes to see, feet to move around and so on. But each organ is not called Narasimha Swamiji. All of them are part and parcel of the whole concept that is Narasimha Swamiji. When you think of Narasimha Swamiji it is only one form. It is the sum total of all these organs in one individual. This individual has one full personality and an objective. When we accept the whole concept do we consider the different parts as the individual?" Smt.Sharada's doubt was cleared at once.

Since Sri O.K.Varada Rao was a Law graduate, under the guidance of Narasimha Swamiji, he prepared the articles and memorandum for the constitution of the All India Sai Samaj. He also laid down the various policies and procedures for the day to day administration of the organization. He also actively took part in Sai prachar work and was instrumental in several youngsters joining the All India Sai Samaj.

Sri Varada Rao proudly used to recall how Narasimha Swamiji had erased his 'self' in all his activities. In all the books published by the All India Sai Samaj, Swamiji used the caption 'no rights reserved' so that anybody anywhere could use the contents freely and without any prior approval. Once it so happened that Sri Varada Rao with his legal background unknowingly had got the words 'All rights reserved' printed. Narasimha Swamiji did not like this and asked Sri Varada Rao to correct it to read as 'No rights reserved' before dispatching the books. Somehow due to work pressure he could not do it. In the evening when he came back to the Sai Samaj office, he was shocked to see Narasimha Swamiji himself incorporating the corrections! Sri Varada Rao used to recall this incident while paying glowing tributes to Narasimha Swamiji's selflessness in all aspects.

Lockets and calendars

Narasimha Swamiji arranged for printing of Sai Baba's pictures on a mass scale. These pictures were useful for creating devotion for Sai Baba.

Rao Brothers, Printers in Triplicane, Madras, produced pictures of Sai Baba from tricolour blocks on art paper in card size and cabinet size. The Tripurasundari Jewellery works in Mint Street, Madras, made lockets in circular and star designs, in small, medium and big sizes and in gold plate and nickel. Every locket contains a picture of Sai Baba on one side and a deity on the other side. Around the picture of Sai Baba are minted in Tamil the famous saying of Sai Baba – 'Why fear when I am there'. They also made rings, buttons and pendants containing Sai Baba's figure in bust and tiny silver *padukas*. Devotees were quite enthusiastic in purchasing these items. This generated a lot of income for the All India Sai Samaj, which in turn was helpful in its expansion. Today Sai Baba's pictures, lockets, rings are quite common and are seen in every household, but one should remember their origin at Madras under the leadership of Narasimha Swamiji. Swamiji introduced these items even at Shirdi, as none of them were available there prior to 1941. Lockets and rings were supplied to Shirdi from Madras suppliers even up to 1970.

When Narasimha Swamiji went to Shirdi for the first time in 1936, the number of persons seeking solace at the feet of Sai Baba could be counted. Even though thousands used to flock to Shirdi when Sai Baba was in physical form, after his 'Mahasamadhi' the number of visitors had drastically reduced to a single digit and even intimate devotees of Sai Baba were under the impression that Sai Baba's glory like that of any other mortal had reached the peak which had come down after his casting the mortal coil. It was only after 1936, the Sai movement led by Narasimha Swamiji gathered tremendous momentum spreading all over the country and reaching out even beyond the frontiers of India. Today not hundreds but millions visit Shirdi to have 'darshan' of Sai Baba.

But this was not an easy task. Even though he had contributed wholeheartedly in taking Sai Baba to all nooks and corners of India, he had to face a lot of resistance. Many were hostile to him engaging in anti-propaganda, 'This man wants us to worship a Muslim fakhir'. Since the All India Sai Samaj was getting a huge income from sale of lockets, rings etc., even a few among the authorities of Shirdi Samsthan were jealous of Narasimha Swamiji. They went to the extent of inserting press releases and notices in the newspapers – 'This Madrasi Sadhu is doing all this for gaining money. Nobody should believe him'.

Very soon, some important people at Shirdi realized that Narasimha Swamiji's efforts were wholehearted and sincere and they encouraged the Sai movement. Undaunted by all this anti-propaganda, Narasimha Swamiji also continued his Sai *prachar* work with the firm conviction 'When Sai Baba is with me, why should I be afraid of anything.' The opposition to Narasimha Swamiji and the anti-propaganda for Sai prachar work came to an end very soon and even his detractors co-operated with Swamiji, after realizing his selfless service to take 'Sai Baba out of Shirdi to all over'.

Narasimha Swamiji realized that all these trials and tribulations were only to test his firm faith in achieving his objective and he was fully aware that Sai Baba had accepted his mission. During his Sai prachar work, on many occasions he referred to this aspect and he had referred to the manifold miracles he experienced in his discourses and articles.

Narasimha Swamiji's immense and matchless efforts have discovered for us Sai Baba as a world saviour whose presence in our hearts helps us to ward off danger and cast off fear. To some extent it is true that the rapid spread of Sai faith was due to the emphasis, which was laid on the mundane benefits derived from devotion to Sai Baba.

But it is mainly through conferring material benefits that God always attracts and draws devotees to Himself, secures their love and devotion and places them on the path that leads them to their moral and spiritual advancement. Were He not "our refuge and strength, our helper amid the flood of mortal ills prevailing", nobody would care for God.

Narasimha Swamiji has stated in his work *Life of Sai Baba* – Vol. I, that at the time of his 'Mahasamadhi in 1918, Sai Baba was little understood and there was hardly anything worth calling a real account of his life. Even in 1936, hardly ten people used to visit the shrine, but it was only after 1936, the Sai movement gathered momentum spreading all over India and even abroad. The rise and spread of the Sai movement is entirely due to the initiative and devoted and single-minded endeavour of Narasimha Swamiji. To say this is to state the obvious. But we need to remind ourselves of the immense debt of gratitude we owe to Narasimha Swamiji for showing us Lord Sainath, the Saviour, and leading us to Him.

Sri Narasimha Swamiji's residence near Sri Lakshmi Narayana Perumal temple in Salem where he used to live before building his bungalow in Salem Extension.

Sri Narasimha Swamiji, a leading Advocate of Salem at the peak of his career.

Sri Lakshmi Narayan Perumal Temple in Salem Agraharam which was renovated by Sri Narasimha Swamiji.

Sri Narasimha Swamiji's bungalow in Salem Extension

Early days at Sri Ramana Ashram

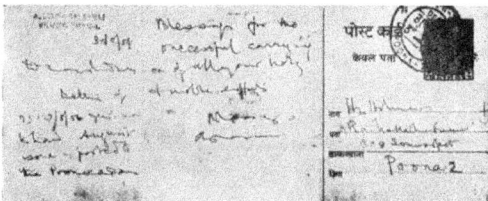

A copy of Sri Narasimha Swamiji's letter to Sri Radhakrishna Swamiji.

Bhagwan Sri Ramana Maharishi of
Sri Arunachala Kshetra (Tiruvannamalai)

Cottage near the cave in Tiruvannamalai, built by
Sri Narasimha Swamiji during his stay there.
This is now known as Sri Paul Brunton Cottage.

Cave at the rear of Sri Ramana Ashram in
Tiruvannamalai where Sri Narasimha Swamiji used
to do his sadhana during his three-year sojourn.

Self Realization, a book written
by Sri Narasimha Swamiji on
Sri Ramana Maharishi

The President of the Raman Ashram
Trust and Sri Radhakrishna Swamiji at
Bhagavan Ramana Maharishi's
Samadhi in Tiruvannamalai.

Rear portion of the cave in Tiruvannamalai
where Sri Narasimha Swamiji used
to do his *sadhana*.

Skand Ashram

Seshadri Swami

Kavyakanta Ganapathy Sastry

Sri Narayan Maharaj of Khedgaonbet
near Poona where Sri Narasimha Swamiji
received spiritual direction.

Upasini Maharaj and Godavari Mata of Sakori

Upasini Ashram, Sakori

This is the place in the All India Sai Samaj Mandir Hall, Madras (Chennai), where Sri Narasimha Swamiji used to sit in his easy-chair.

Sri Narasimha Swamiji's portrait placed in the Dhyana Mandir of All India Sai Samaj, Mylapore, Madras (Chennai)

Gurupurnima Day celebration in 1946 at Dr. Nanjunda Rao's house in Mylapore, Madras (Chennai) where Sri Narasimha Swamiji blessed the devotees.

Picture of Sri Narasimha Swamiji taken when he addressed a congregation in 1946 about Sri Sai Baba's greatness.

Sri Narasimha Swamiji after a *pada* puja in 1948

Dr. Nanjunda Rao

Shirdi Sai Baba's statue, All India Sai Samaj, Mylapore, Madras (Chennai).

Dr. G.R.Vijayakumar, author of English book giving rare copies of 'Sai Leela' to Dr. Rabinder Nath Kakarya (Hindi Translator) (2007)

Sri Radhakrishna Swamiji (left) and
Sri Narasimha Swamiji (Right)
in Tumkur in Mysore State
during Sai Prachar Work.

P.R. Aavasti

M.V. Pradhan

M. B. Rege

Das Ganu Maharaj

Govind Ragunath Dhabolkar
(Hemadpant)

Sri Narasimha Swamiji
as he looked in 1940
when he was engaged
in Sai Prachar work.

The Sage of Sakuri, A book by
Sri Narasimha Swamiji on Upasani Baba.

Shiv Linga and Nandi installed outside
Maruti Mandir by
Sri Narasimha Swamiji (Shirdi)

Lord Dattatreya

Gajanan Maharaj (Shegaon)

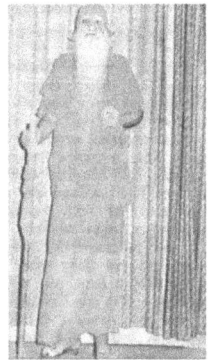

Ram Baba

Ajmer Sharif (Khwaja Moinuddin
Chisty Dargah Sharif)

ताजुदीन वली.
वाकी.

Tajuddin Baba

Meher Baba

Pushkar Tirth (Rajasthan)

Abdul Baba

Sri Narasimha Swamiji (with a book in hand) at Ramana Maharishi Ashram.

Lectures and discourses

Narasimha Swamiji gave a clarion call – "Journals must be multiplied in various languages and books must be published... gatherings, lectures and kirtans should be held all over the county. Poojas and bhajans must be arranged everywhere everyday. Sai Baba must permeate the country from one end to another." This was his goal and he achieved it in toto.

On one side, Narasimha Swamiji was publishing books on Sai Baba in different languages. At the same time he was travelling all over the country addressing people on Sai Baba. Some times alone, and at times accompanied by local people or volunteers, Narasimha Swamiji covered all the nooks and corners of the country lecturing, organizing, founding new Samajams, inaugurating Sai worship in individual houses, counselling people to steady the wandering minds to concentrate on Sai Baba, to chant the mantra 'Sai Ram' and integrating several into one large and common brotherhood bound by their single hearted devotion and loyalty to Sai Baba. He travelled by third class in railways, by bullock carts, *jutkas*, buses, motorcars, accepting any place to rest, living on plain fare or choice dishes, whatever came to him. He carried *udhi*; Sai Baba's pictures in card size, and *Sai Ashtotharam* for free distribution. He never worried whether his audiences were large or small. He addressed students, women and men pursuing various vocations, teachers, traders, artists, artisans and craftsmen. He spoke in houses, clubs, schools, in parks and public places. His clear and ringing tone reached them all bringing a message of hope and good cheer and opening a new chapter, a bright page in their lives. He is still remembered with affection and gratitude for this.

Between 1940 and 1950 he covered nearly all the principal towns now form a part of Tamil Nadu, Andhra Pradesh, Karnataka and Kerala. In 1943, he lectured in Bombay and Bhusaval. He addressed meetings in Delhi, Allahabad, Benaras and Kolkata. He covered the Theosophical Society and the Central Hindu College in Benaras and the Ramakrishna Institute of Culture in Kolkata. He spoke in Ahmedabad and formed a Sai Samaj there. Between 1940 and 1943, he was invited thrice to Kolkata to vitalize a strong Sai Samaj there. He went to Kharagpur and in Assam he covered Masimpur, Karimganj and Silchar. In Bihar, he visited Patna and Jamshedpur in his lecture tours.

By these lecture tours he built a network of *Upasamajams*. By 1946, sixty-five *Upasamajams* spread all over India and affiliated to the All India Sai Samaj were in operation. Fifteen Sai Mandirs were built in various towns. Narasimha Swamiji planned his tours in advance and published the itinerary in the 'Sai Sudha' magazine. After his lecture tours, local devotees and organisers sent reports of his work for publication.

At this stage there occurred interesting happenings that promoted the Sai movement. Those who took to Sai worship reported the miracles, which have made Sai Baba so popular. The early issues of Sai Sudha contained several reports of this nature. At the initial stages of the movement, demand grew steadily for Sai literature and Sai gifts such as rings, lockets, pendants etc., and also the *udhi* Swamiji had brought from Shirdi. It became necessary to formulate a systematic way of conducting Sai worship. Accordingly, Narasimha Swamiji has given 'Sai Pooja Vidhi' and 'Sai Sahasranama' in addition to the *ashtotharam* already in use. This is published in Sanskrit, Tamil, Telugu and Kannada. Pooja was offered to tiny silver *padukas*, lockets and to Sai Baba's pictures.

Narasimha Swamiji composed in Sanskrit, hymns under the title 'Sainatha Mananam', which enables a devotee to have instant contemplation on Sai Baba. It has been transliterated into Tamil and English.

One important incident, which occurred on 7th January, 1943 at Coimbatore, gave a boost to the Sai movement. On that day, a king cobra bearing marks of conch and wheel on its hood appeared before Sai Baba's picture during the bhajans conducted in a *shamiana* on a vacant plot receiving flowers from the growing congregation. The cobra was photographed and offered milk. Crowds rushed to that area to see this miracle. After staying amidst the devotees for more than twenty-four hours, the cobra crawled into an anthill in the neighbourhood. The devotees were thrilled to see Sai Baba giving 'darshan' in the form of a king cobra. Sri A.Varadarajaiah bought that vacant plot and with the help of other devotees built a temple for Sai Baba there, which is famous as the 'Naga Sai Mandir'.

The news of the miracle at Coimbatore spread like a wildfire and thousands joined the Sai movement. Narasimha Swamiji was the torchbearer of the message of Sai Baba and the Sai movement grew in leaps and bounds.

Meeting the disciple

Sai Baba had to wait for eighteen years for a suitable disciple who could spread his message. But it was a different case with Narasimha Swamiji. He did not have to wait for a long time to secure a worthy disciple who could enthusiastically carry on his Mission. The disciple he selected was a young and dynamic person, Sri K.Radhakrishnan who was at Ooty. He later on evolved himself into Sri Saipadananda Radhakrishna Swamiji and took over the leadership of the Sai movement from Narasimha Swamiji.

The Guru-Sishya meeting itself was in dramatic circumstances in a most unexpected way. It had been announced in Ooty by a citizen's committee that Narasimha Swamiji, Founder and President of the All India Sai Samaj, would address a meeting on Sai Baba. The meeting was to be held in a school (St. Joseph's Matriculation School, Ooty) and the organisers, who were Radhakrishnan's friends, had asked him to remain inside the building while they went out to receive the visitor. Radhakrishnan had not intended to attend the meeting; he had planned to watch a movie, *David Livingstone*.

In deference to the wishes of his friends, he stayed on and to his great surprise very soon he found a bearded saintly person enter the school hall all alone. He realized the visitor must be Narasimha Swamiji, who had come by an unscheduled route to the meeting place. He told Narasimha Swamiji that the organisers were waiting outside on the main road to receive him. "Oh, never mind," was

Narasimha Swamiji's response. "The bus was delayed. So to make up lost time I came by a different road. Now it is already 6.30 pm. I do not like to delay any further. What! Are you ready?" Radhakrishnan mechanically said, "Yes", although he did not know what he was expected to do. Narasimha Swamiji took out a picture of Sai Baba from his bag and placed it on a chair. Radhakrishnan understood he was required to do the pooja. But he felt embarrassed because he was dressed in a suit and told Narasimha Swamiji: "I am wearing a suit. At least, I should be wearing a dhoti…" He was not allowed to complete the sentence. Narasimha Swamiji laughed and said : "It does not matter at all. Sai Baba never looks at the external details. What he wants is the mind. You do the pooja." Radhakrishnan found himself in a ticklish situation. He could not do anything without telling his friends, nor could he refuse to carry out the instructions of one who appeared to be a saint. He finally performed the pooja. Afterwards at the end of the meeting, he did the 'Mangal-Arathi' also.

Radhakrishnan took Narasimha Swamiji to his house in Fernhill, Ooty, where his eldest brother, Sri V.S.Rajagopala Aiyer and his family were presented to him. Narasimha Swamiji installed a Sai Baba idol in the house and worshipped it. Later, Rajagopala Aiyer was put in charge of the Sai Baba Mandir at Ooty and he became a member of the All India Sai Samaj. Radhakrishnan escorted Narasimha Swamiji to the bus stand on his way back and it was then he put a very crucial question to him. "Swamiji, I have a peculiar feeling. I feel the name a person gets in this world has some deeper meaning behind it. I have been named Radhakrishnan but I do not clearly follow why I got this name." (According to Radhakrishnan's family circles, the name was given to him since he was born after his mother had attended a Radha Kalyan discourse).

Narasimha Swamiji thought for a while and then said: "If you really want to know the meaning of Radhakrishna, I will let you know, but you come and stay in Madras." Narasimha Swamiji had already told Radhakrishnan's brother that he wanted men of the caliber of Radhakrishnan to help him in spreading Sai Baba's message and Rajagopala Aiyer had agreed that Radhakrishnan should join Narasimha Swamiji in Madras.

The young devotee, Radhakrishnan, started reading literature connected with Sai Baba, but he was disappointed that there was no good book available in English giving complete details about the life and teachings of Sai Baba. He learnt that the material for writing an exhaustive biography had been collected after years of research and patience by Narasimha Swamiji. Radhakrishnan had already read a remarkable book by Narasimha Swamiji, 'Self Realisation – a biography of Sri Ramana Maharishi' about which he said: "So complete was the attunement of the author with the subject of his study that the book compelled my admiration and I got absorbed in it." However, he was nagged by a doubt which was - how was it that a person like Narasimha Swamiji who had the benefit of personal contact with a living sage of the eminence of Sri Ramana Maharishi, had been drawn towards Sai Baba, a saint who was no more and whose method of teaching differed considerably from that of Sri Ramana Maharishi?"

Strangely enough, Radhakrishnan found that Narasimha Swamiji was at that very moment in Ooty and he sought an interview with him to clear his doubt. Narasimha Swamiji explained to him at some length the circumstances and reasons which had guided his footsteps in his search for a final resting place where his heart could abide in complete faith, with a mind which is in repose because it is no longer assailed by doubts.

It is not known when exactly Radhakrishnan came to Madras after he accepted Narasimha Swamiji as his Guru. It might have been sometime in 1943 or 44. He lived with a family in George Town for some time and then in a room in the auditor's firm in which he worked. It was while staying with a couple that he had a remarkable spiritual experience, which had a profound effect on him. After his first meeting with Narasimha Swamiji he was thirsting to know the meaning of Radhakrishnan, which his Guru had promised would be revealed to him if he came to Madras.

After some days he took a vow that he would not eat until the Lord revealed himself to him to show the significance of Radhakrishna. He started fasting. On the second day he ran high temperature and the couple with whom he was staying were worried and called in a doctor. But he would not take the medicine prescribed and continued his fast. On the third day he had *darshan* of Radha and Krishna. This was how he has described it: "I was lying in an easy chair on the terrace of the house and was wide awake. I was praying to Radha: 'Mother, you have to show Him to me soon'. Suddenly I saw a bright light in the sky. Gradually I perceived the light to be none other than Radha, who appeared to be an 18-year old girl. After a while Krishna came in the same way and they stood in front of me hugging each other as you see in the traditional pictures and idols. Radha was holding me by one hand and Krishna by another. She took me nearer to Krishna and said:' This is Krishna'. Then the vision disappeared. My fever began to subside. It was a great vision. I had actually prayed to Radha to show me Krishna and this had proved effective."

Radhakrishnan had another experience, which revealed to him who Sai Baba was. One day Sai Baba told him: "Read the tenth." He could not say if it was in a dream or in a vision. He mentioned this to Narasimha Swamiji and added that perhaps Sai Baba wanted him to read the tenth book of the Bhagavatham. But his Guru told him he thought Sai Baba had meant the tenth chapter of the Bhagvadgita, which refers to *Vibhuti yoga*. Radhakrishnan started reading the tenth chapter of the Gita.

One night as he was lying in the open at the All India Sai Samaj premises he suddenly saw the entire sky filled with the various forms of Gods and Goddesses, including Krishna, Rama etc., He prayed to Sai Baba: "Oh, Sai Baba, I do not want all these. I want to know your real form, who you are and that alone. Please show that to me." All the forms in the sky vanished and only those of Sri Rama and Maruthi remained. Radhakrishnan exclaimed: "It then became clear to me that Sai Baba and Rama are one and the same. I told Narasimha Swamiji about this and he was happy to hear of this experience and said: 'So it is definite Sai and Rama are the same'."

Referring to this Radhakrishnan said: "You see, Sai Baba did not say, 'I am Rama'. He just showed Rama. This indicated I thought that Sai Baba was a great Rama Bhakta. In Sai Satcharita you might have read about his eagerness to celebrate Sri Rama Navami. Also whenever he saw a Maruthi temple he would jump in ecstasy. This is the characteristic of a true *bhakta*."

It is not certain when Radhakrishnan broke off all family bonds after he settled in Madras. There was pressure from his people to return home. His close relations used all means to persuade him to change his mind. They also approached Narasimha Swamiji to intervene. But Radhakrishnan was adamant and they had to give up their efforts. He gave up the job of steward of the Race Club, worked in an auditor's firm and later became a director of the Mylapore Permanent Fund. Outwardly he was a handsome young man, neatly dressed in a clean dhoti and white *jubba* with an upper cloth thrown over one shoulder. Those days, he gave an impression as the one who was extremely attentive to his appearance and manners. He was a voracious reader and his favourite haunt was the Theosophical Society Library at Adyar where he spent many hours pouring over religious and occult literature. At the Theosophical Society gardens he found a quiet place to meditate under a tree.

A Sanskrit book, *Mantra Mahodari* was always to be found in Radhakrishnan's hands those days. The book was a mine of information on *japas* and mantras prescribed by the sages of yore to achieve various *siddhis*. T.Kesava Rao and V.K.Panthulu were close associates of Radhakrishnan. They would not do anything connected with the All India Sai Samaj without consulting each other.

Radhakrishnan supervised the accounts of the Samaj and helped Narasimha Swamiji in other ways in his personal and public work. Narasimha Swamiji put him in charge of the library and he would always be found surrounded by books, very happy and contented.

Radhakrishnan was a person who never pushed himself up. He was physically much better built than in his later days and he was an 'impressive figure'. His surrender to Narasimha Swamiji was total and whatever Narasimha Swamiji said was law to him.

Radhakrishnan acted as liaison in legal and other work connected with the All India Sai Samaj. He spent most of his time in the Samaj premises when he was not busy otherwise. Every evening Narasimha Swamiji used to ask Radhakrishnan to read verses from the Gita and he would explain their meaning to the assembled devotees. It was on one such occasion that in Narasimha Swamiji's presence that Radhakrishnan recited *Vishnu Sahasranamam*, which became so much a part of his divine mission later on. By 1946, these discourses became rare, as Narasimha Swamiji was busy with the fast expanding activities of the All India Sai Samaj.

Radhakrishnan was a dynamic young man but was never showy. He always remained in the background. He used to avoid photographs too in public functions of the Samaj.

Radhakrishnan was deputed by Narasimha Swamiji to Shirdi for liaison with the Shirdi Samsthan on his behalf and to ensure proper facilities for pilgrims from the South. He later became a member of the Shirdi Samsthan Committee. Narasimha Swamiji sent him on Sai prachar work to many centers in North India and this entailed long separation from his Guru, which became permanent when he was asked to go to Bangalore in 1952 for Sai prachar.

About his itinerant life, Radhakrishnan has reminisced as follows: - "I was leading a comfortable life in Ooty. Then my contact with Narasimha Swamiji brought me to Madras. Swamiji gave me a plank of wood to sleep on and I had to sleep on that plank without a pillow, using one of my arms as a pillow. You see from the comfort, which I enjoyed at Ooty what hardship I had to undergo in Madras. This was a test. God will enter us only when we maintain equanimity of mind whether it is 'sukha' or 'dukha'. Right from the day I started following Narasimha Swamiji I have found that Sai Baba puts one through a number of tests and even hardships. He put me in Bombay, Shirdi and later at Bangalore, depriving me completely of my contact with my Guru. I became unhappy but later felt it was His will and should be quietly followed. All these Sai Baba will do to make one evolve as a devotee. He will go on giving such tests until one passes them successfully. The essence of 'Bhakti marga' is this. And when once the Lord through *bhakti* takes a person, he is taken forever. The Lord will never forsake him."

Narasimha Swamiji sent Radhakrishna Swamiji to Bangalore in 1952 for 'Sai prachar' work in old Mysore area. In 1953, Narasimha Swamiji gave the title 'Saipadananda' to his devoted disciple. Radhakrishna Swamiji is the greatest gift of Narasimha Swamiji to the public of Karnataka in general and Bangalore in particular. He established Sri Sai Spiritual Centre and attracted thousands of devotees to the Sai Marg. We are eternally grateful to Narasimha Swamiji for blessing us with a Sadguru like Radhakrishna Swamiji.

Ef cient system for Sai Prachar

⟢

In 1941, Narasimha Swamiji founded an organization named 'All India Sai Samaj with headquarters at Madras to serve as the centre of activities of the Sai movement. During his tour in various towns several people became his followers and with the guidance of Narasimha Swamiji they started Sai Samajams, which were called *Upasamajams* affiliated to the main body, the All India Sai Samaj. With no place of its own to function from, the All India Sai Samaj was first housed in a small rented room in Venkatachala Mudali Street, Triplicane, Madras. On 13th April 1942, the Samaj moved to a house in T.S.V.Koil Street, Mylapore, Madras. This house was considered to be a haunted place and was therefore readily available to accommodate Sai Baba and Narasimha Swamiji. With their arrival, ghosts haunting that place should have got liberated! With the blessings of Swamiji two 'Bhajan Mandalis' came into existence –

1. The Narasimha Swamiji Dwarakamayi Prathama Sishya Ghosti headed by S.Sundareswara Iyer of the Railways,

2. The Triplicane Sai Bhajan Mandali led by C.R.Narasimha Raghavan.

In January 1943, the office of the All India Sai Samaj moved to 126, Brodies Road, Madras. Literature, pictures, lockets, rings etc., were sold from the Central Sai Stores at this address. Even upto 1970 shops in Shirdi received their supplies of lockets, rings etc, from Madras.

Till a permanent building for the All India Sai Samaj was constructed in 1953, Narasimha Swamiji had evolved an efficient system for the propagation of the Sai movement. Each Thursday devotees would gather in the house of one chosen devotee by turn. On each occasion Narasimha Swamiji would present a picture of Sai Baba to the host of the day. There would be bhajan and 'Nama Sankirtan' followed by a talk by Narasimha Swamiji extolling Sai 'Mahima'. That was the humble and simple way in which he carried on the Sai bhakti movement, gathering sincere devotees in mere handfuls here and there.

Both Sai Baba and Narasimha Swamiji must have got tired of their itinerant life and Swamiji longed for a permanent abode for Sai Baba in Madras. Around this time, a house in Mylapore had fallen vacant, the tenant having vacated it in a hurry when he found a dead cat in it. When this information was passed on to Narasimha Swamiji, he jumped at the idea and occupied the house without a moment's hesitation.

When it was found that this house was not sufficient for the increasing number of devotees that were gathering for bhajans, particularly on Thursdays, Narasimha Swamiji moved over to the house of Dr.Nanjunda Rao in September 1943, on the North Mada Street in Mylapore, now known as Ramakrishna Mutt Road.

In January 1949, when Dr.Nanjunda Rao's grandson retired from service and wanted the house back for his own occupation; Narasimha Swamiji began to look for another suitable place for Sai Baba. At this time an advocate, Sri Thyagarajan offered the use of the open space in front of his house in Venkatesha Agraharam. A pucca pandal was put up here and All India Sai Samaj shifted here in January 1949.

Narasimha Swamiji now planned to have a permanent abode to house the All India Sai Samaj. With the donations received in response to his appeal he was able to buy a vast extent of land in the same road to the west of the location from where the Samaj was functioning. The plot was purchased for Rs.29, 770/- in 1949.

Narasimha Swamiji began construction of a temple for Sai Baba at the newly acquired site. When the construction was in progress, on 'Guru Poornima' day – 7th July, 1952, Swamiji shifted the Samaj to the new site. The main temple with 'Garbagriha' and tower were ready in October 1953. Narasimha Swamiji's ambition was fulfilled and *Mahakumbhabhishekam* was performed on 19th October 1953. Regular worship began in the new Sai Mandir. With the funds available only a zinc-sheet-roofed open hall could be constructed in front of the shrine for devotees to sit and stand and offer pooja.

In 1954, land measuring approximately ten grounds to the west of the Sai Mandir came up for sale through court. Since this area would be very useful for expanding the humanitarian activities of the All India Sai Samaj, Narasimha Swamiji acquired this place too with great difficulty. A spacious hall with a stage called 'Sai Kala Mantap' rose up here in 1955 which was used for arranging lectures, cultural programmes etc., In this manner, a big building was raised on this ground in a phased manner even though by 1953 itself, the All India Sai Samaj had a permanent structure.

Between 1944 and 1950, the All India Sai Samaj published calendars containing Sai Baba's pictures in tricolour from time to time and priced at five annas only. The Library was opened on Vijaya Dashami in 1944. Radhakrishnan was put in charge of the library and by his untiring efforts put in a good foundation for a library with a very good collection of books.

By then Narasimha Swamiji had taken up extensive tours all over the country and had spread the message of Sai Baba to the nooks and corners. By 1950 he had built seventy-five *Upasamajams* affiliated to the All India Sai Samaj and a network of thousands of sincere Sai devotees. Over fifteen Sai Baba temples were built all over India as a result of Narasimha Swamiji's extensive tours and many more were under construction. A band of volunteers readily assisted him in Sai prachar work and Sai Baba, who was confined only to Shirdi uptil 1936, had now moved over to the entire country.

During his extensive trips on Sai prachar work, Narasimha Swamiji was a victim of accidents. In May 1943, a bullock cart hit him as he was crossing a road in Vani Vilas Mohalla of Mysore. He was wounded in the left forearm and right foot. His companion got his collar bone fractured. They were hospitalized till June 13, 1943 and then sent to Madras.

Like this, he sustained fractures on seven occasions. But he welcomed each accident as 'Sai's will' and a way to alleviate his bad 'Karma'. He used to rest for a while and the moment he used to get better, again start off on his whirlwind trips of Sai prachar. We still see old photographs showing Narasimha Swamiji in plaster casts and delivering lectures on Sai Baba.

Slides were made to depict the life and work of Sai Baba. On Saturday evenings from March 1953, lantern lectures were organised along with bhajans at the All India Sai Samaj premises. Sri P. Gopalaswamy delivered lantern lectures in some places in Tiruchirapalli and in Maharashtra. Sai Sudha announced the readiness of the All India Sai Samaj to help *Upasamajams* by sending lantern lecturers with equipment for Sai prachar.

Narasimha Swamiji introduced onto the pattern of Shirdi the three Sai festivals, namely, Sri Rama Navami, Guru Poornima, Baba's Mahasamadhi anniversary. *Laksharchanas*, bhajans, devotional music, spiritual discourses and feeding the poor called 'Narayana Seva' formed the common programme of these festivals. He inspired the *Upasamajams* by sending them messages for each occasion. At the headquarters, Rama Navami and Mahasamadhi anniversary were observed for ten days by organizing musical entertainments every evening. Vidwans Papanasam Sivam, Dandapani Desikar, Maharajapuram Viswanatha Iyer and other artistes gave free performances. Banni Bai and other artistes presented *Katha Kalakshepams* and *Hari Kathas*. They drew crowds by their talents and helped in publicity. Since 1953, Sai festivals included *Ratha Yatra* – processions on the main streets in the vicinity.

Narasimha Swamiji had not neglected the writing part of his work. He produced early in 1944 a play in seven acts in Tamil titled 'Sri Sai Charita Natakam'. Two others namely, A.S.Narasimhan and Narasimha Dasan also wrote plays on Sai Baba's life. The Triplicane Dramatic Society, the Rasika Ranjani Sabha and other artists associations at Madras and other places in Tamil Nadu put these plays on board. The income generated was quite good and useful for furthering Sai prachar.

Narasimha Swamiji also wrote 'Sai Harikatha' to help those who sought to popularize the Sai movement by performing stories on Sai Baba with music. Sai Harikatha enabled rural people to understand Sai Baba faster.

Narasimha Swamiji commenced his great task of writing a detailed biography of Sai Baba in English by publishing the first volume in March 1943. Volume II was published in July 1956. Although the manuscript was ready, Volume III was published in July 1957 and Volume IV in 1969 as posthumous works.

In January 1945, he published the *Glimpses of Sai Baba* with a foreword by Justice Sri C.N.Kuppuswamy Iyer. In this work, Narasimha Swamiji corrects the popular notion about Sai Baba that he is only a miracle worker who delights in granting material favours to his devotees. The author has brought out how in every one of his actions and dealings with his devotees; Sai Baba always had prominently in his mind the spiritual welfare of those devotees. In this book, Narsimha Swamiji has been able to throw a flood of light on the inner meaning of Baba's sayings and doings.

In the midst of his lecture tours and turning out Sai literature, Narasimha Swamiji also attended to his official duties. He disposed off correspondence, granted interviews, presided over committee meetings and annual general meetings and directed the daily activities at the headquarters. One can gain an idea of how much he was handling from the following extract taken from page 6 of 'Sai Sudha' – April 1945 : -

"The President finds himself unable to cope with the increasing pressure of work...organization of the *Upasamajams* and Mandirs and supervision of the matter for Sai Sudha are quite enough to keep all his time and energy...The institution suffers no less than the individual by concentration of all work on an old pair of shoulders."

Narasimha Swamiji was doing everything – travel, correspondence, writing etc., - all by himself. Had it been a Government activity, a separate department would have been created. A separate University would not have undertaken the writing work he had completed. He used to direct the activities of *Upasamajams* himself. He used to send them messages periodically. He used to reply to each and every letter addressed to him. On an average he used to work for 18 to 20 hours a day. Though his body had worn out, he was a dynamic young man at heart.

In January 1946, the idea of holding an All India Sai Devotees' Convention was mooted by Narasimha Swamiji. The movement grew out of the local *Upasamajams*, which in turn looked for inspiration and guidance from Narasimha Swamiji and his group of volunteers. It became necessary therefore for a conference to be held between the delegates of *Upasamajams* and Narasimha Swamiji or a body of volunteers deputed by the headquarters. This conference was planned as an annual feature to discuss problems of organization and concert measures to strengthen and expand the Sai movement.

Accordingly, after careful preparations the first All India Sai Devotees' Convention was organised on 16th, 17th, 18th and 19th May 1946 at the P.S.High School, Madras. Two hundred delegates registered from outside and several local devotees attended. The proceedings opened daily, with prayer and service in the forenoon at the All India Sai Samaj. The afternoon sessions were held at the Convention Hall in the P.S.High School, Mylapore.

Narasimha Swamiji as President of the All India Sai Samaj was elected President of the Convention and also Chairman of the Reception Committee. The Convention opened in the afternoon of the 16th May 1946 after prayers in Sanskrit, Tamil, Telugu and Hindi. It is interesting to note that Narasimha Swamiji while welcoming the delegates, referred to shortages of foodgrains, fuel, electricity, petrol and paper. He requested the delegates to accept whatever plain food was offered to them. He exhorted them to include 'Narayana Seva' (feeding the poor) in the activities of their *Upasamajams* and to work for communal harmony and brotherhood.

Among the messages of greetings received from those were from Rao Bahadur M.W.Pradhan and Justice Sri M.B.Rege, who had personal contact with Sai Baba. Das Ganu Maharaj, Marthand Mhalsapathy and Swami Keshavaiah participated actively in the convention. Delegates discussed the activities of their *samajams* and problems and devotees narrated their experiences.

Resolutions were passed in line with the Presidential address. As started in Coimbatore by the Sai Baba Mission, it was also resolved that each *Upasamajam* should think in terms of starting Sai Baba Gurukulams, Kanya Vidyalaya and Narasimha Ashramams to extend educational facilities and medical relief for the destitute, poor and needy. The Convention also noted with appreciation the working of the Sai Baba High School started by S.Adinarayana Rao at Ananthapur in Andhra Pradesh in 1944. Narasimha Swamiji outlined his plans of starting a free dispensary and a school at Samaj premises for the use of slum dwellers and other poor and downtrodden people.

The cultural programme of the convention included music, Sai Harikatha in Tamil and Telugu and a Telugu drama based on the life of Sai Baba.

The session closed in the afternoon on 19th May 1946 with 'Narayana Seva' organised at the backyard of 136, Brodies Road. More than one thousand persons were served food.

A copiously illustrated Souvenir, printed on art paper of the size of 'Sai Sudha' and priced at 8 annas a copy was brought out.

Publishing Convention Souvenirs of larger size has come into practice ever since.

The first All India Sai Devotees' Convention set the pattern for other conventions held in later years. Narasimha Swamiji's age and declining health precluded him from attending subsequent conventions, which were held far away from Madras. But he sent messages to all these conventions. The impetus given to the movement by these Conventions is beyond description. It became popular year by year and the network of Sai devotees widened.

The Convention of Sai Devotees, which started in 1946, became an annual feature. At Coimbatore in 1947, at Madurai in 1949, at Kolkata in 1950, at Dharwar in 1951, at Pune in 1952, at Mumbai in 1953, at Baroda in 1954, the conventions were a great success and devotees were looking forward to these conventions eagerly. These conventions have enabled millions to join the Sai marg. Narasimha Swamiji was happy that the movement he started had taken gigantic proportions and was continuously growing.

By then at the Alamelu Mangapuram sector of Venkatesha Agraharam in Madras, a plot was purchased and a temporary shed was built. By donations from generous devotees, due to a powerful appeal in Sai Sudha and sale of Sai literature, funds were raised to complete the building of the front hall. Here Sai Baba's picture was installed and worshipped on 'Guru Poornima' day on 7th July, 1952. By October 1953, construction of the temple with a tower on the model at Shirdi was completed.

On 9th September 1953, the Maharaja of Mysore, H.H. Sri Jayachamaraja Wodeyar visited the Sai Mandir and donated Rs. 5000/-, which helped the Samaj buy a printing press.

The *Maha Kumbhabhishekam* of the temple was fixed on 18th October 1953 during the 'Mahasamadhi' celebrations. The programmes started with *Sri Sai Laksharchana* and several *homas*. On 17th and 18th 'Guru Aradhana' was held by feeding many devotees and fakhirs. The *Kalasha Stapana* was performed on the 18th and the function closed with procession of Sai Baba with music and fireworks.

The joy of the celebrations was marred by an accident. Earlier to the *Kumbhabhishekam*, Narasimha Swamiji had instructions around 7.30 am from Sai Baba. "You won't be able to perform *Kumbhabhishekam*. So do *Kalasha Pooja* now itself'. Devotees were surprised to see Narasimha Swamiji climbing the ladder to do 'Kalasha Pooja' at 7.30 am itself, when the actual *muhurtham* fixed was at 11 am.

Around 8.30 am, Narasimha Swamiji slipped in the bathroom and broke his thighbone. He was admitted to the Madras Medical College Hospital for treatment. His right thigh was in plaster cast for over eight weeks.

As already indicated to him by Sai Baba, Narasimha Swamiji could not perform *Kumbhabhishekam* and on his behalf Radhakrishna Swamiji performed it and also other rituals connected with it.

Inspite of agonizing pain and immobilization in plaster cast for eight weeks, Narasimha Swamiji did not express this pain on his face. He welcomed this accidental fall as "Sai Baba's will and a way to alleviate past Karma". Sai Baba's *Nama smaran* was constantly on his lips. In fact, he had converted his ward in the hospital to a miniature Sai Mandir.

Narasimha Swamiji's untiring efforts had put the Sai movement on a strong platform. By 1956, All India Sai Samaj had grown by leaps and bounds. It generated a good revenue. Swamiji had groomed a band of dedicated volunteers.

Swamiji's Mahasamadhi

Narasimha Swamiji had laid a firm foundation for the Sai movement by 1956. Sai Baba who was confined only to Shirdi was already known all over India. Even abroad, people were familiar with Sai Baba. The All India Sai Samaj had over four hundred *Upasamajams* affiliated to it. Temples for Sai Baba were constructed all over the country and in 1956, as many as eighty Sai temples were in existence and many more were under construction. Every day the number of devotees worshipping Sai Baba were on the increase and in order to continue the movement started by Narasimha Swamiji thousands and thousands of volunteers got ready. As a worthy successor, Radhakrishna Swamiji was ready to shoulder the leadership of the Sai movement. By then Radhakrishna Swamiji was busily engaged in spreading the Sai movement in Karnataka since 1952.

On 12ᵗʰ September 1956, 83rd birthday of Narasimha Swamiji as per the birth star was celebrated on a low profile at the All India Sai Samaj and other *Upasamajams*. Swamiji's health status was not satisfactory. His physical body had almost worn out. Even by 8ᵗʰ October 1956, he was weak due to fever. He was confined to bed. Even then he directed from his bed various activities like the dictation of the editorial for 'Sai Sudha', attended to office correspondence and meditated when he was free of duties.

In the next seven days, he developed constipation. His limbs grew benumbed and were not even able to move around. He breathed his last and merged in Sai Baba at 3.45 am on 19th October 1956, the day of holy Ashwaija Poornima.

When he attained Mahasamadhi, Narasimha Swamiji transferred all his spiritual powers to Radhakrishna Swamiji, whom he had anointed as his worthy successor. At that time, Radhakrishna Swamiji used to stay in Bangalore. By the evening of 18th October 1956 Radhakrishna Swamiji learnt that the condition of Narasimha Swamiji was quite serious and therefore spent the entire night in meditation. By 4 pm he came out of his meditation and informed his intimate devotees- "My Gurudev Narasimha Swamiji has attained Mahasamadhi just now. As a parting gift he has given away all his spiritual prowess to me." He instructed them to get ready to board the morning train to Madras.

Sai Baba had given away his treasure to Narsimha Swamiji on 29th August 1936 and now this was gifted to Radhakrishna Swamiji. Indeed Radhakrishna Swamiji inherited the three in one treasure - the holy 'Trinity' from 19th October 1956 onwards. Along with a band of devotees Radhakrishna Swamiji left for Madras to take part in the cremation and other final rituals.

Tidings of Narasimha Swamiji's Mahasamadhi spread around quickly and crowds rushed in to pay their respects. Reuter flashed the news over the globe. Telegrams poured in from far and near expressing grief at the heavy loss. Special services were arranged at various temples, headquarters of the All India Sai Samaj and affiliated *Upasamajams*. Condolence meetings were held by Sai devotees at various places all over the country mourning the sad demise of their mentor who showed them who Sai Baba is.

On the evening of 31st October 1956, a public meeting was held at the All India Sai Samaj. Kaviyogi Suddhananda Bharathi Swamiji presided over the meeting. At this memorial service, Radhakrishna Swamiji, Rege Maharaj, Das Ganu Maharaj, Sri K.S.Ramaswamy Shastry, Sri T.M.Krishnaswamy Iyer and other dignitaries paid glowing tributes to the departed Narasimha Swamiji and his services.

Just three weeks before attaining his Mahasamadhi, Narasimha Swamiji had stated in a message :- "In the first place the spiritual leadership of Sai movement is of the utmost importance and none but the Founder amongst the members could provide it. So the Founder still continues to be the spiritual head of the Sai Samaj and of all Sai devotees. It is to facilitate this work that a cottage behind the temple had been erected and allotted to the Founder to live in, and thus become a powerful and always a present guide, director and helper to all."

Even though he has given up his physical body, Narasimha Swamiji is eternally with us. He is answering our prayers. He is guiding us in our spiritual efforts.

The Sai Baba temple and offices of the All India Sai Samaj at 37, Alamelu Mangapuram, Mylapore, Madras, covering about eighteen grounds with the tower rising to a stupendous height and spacious front hall represent in concrete form how much Narasimha Swamiji had achieved by his hard work and sacrifice. We have in this magnificent building a library, hospital and a printing press, community hall for cultural activities, telephone and loudspeaker equipment, living rooms and baths and other amenities of urban life for outstation devotees, feeding poor etc., Whoever comes for 'darshan' is provided 'prasad'. Let us not become lost in these comforts; let us cherish in humility and gratitude the memory of that rare soul for all this. More than seven times he was stricken by accidents; there was division among his followers. Accidents failed to deter him and he put heterogeneous elements together and evolved as His Master Sai Baba had done in Shirdi, 'harmony out of chaos'.

"I find Dwarakamayi here in Madras" declared Justice Sri M.B.Rege as he visited the headquarters of the All India Sai Samaj. He could perceive Sai Baba manifested in that holy atmosphere. He was linked to this place by memory of his close association with Narasimha Swamiji.

Out of over eighty-three years that Narasimha Swamiji had lived, he gave us in the last twenty years the cream of his profound wisdom and scholarship, ripe experience and above all the fruits of his 'tapas'.

Narasimha Swamiji has left us the legacy – the Sai movement and the All India Sai Samaj. We should ask ourselves what we, in turn, have done to preserve and improve that heritage by contributing our share to the work. There is still so much distress around – poverty, ignorance, communal discord, parochialism, selfishness and greed and therefore, so much to do to remove them by carrying the teachings of Sai Baba working in loving memory of Narasimha Swamiji. We may change the situation, however little that change may be. But we must change ourselves first.

Sadguru Narasimha Swamiji is still living in the literature he has left us; literature that goes into so many reprints and gets translated into so many languages, he lives in the 'Ashtotharam' and 'Sahasranamam' he composed and we chant in 'Sai Mananam' and the songs we sing. His spirit is brooding over the cottage behind the temple at the All India Sai Samaj, in the easy chair that held him, nay in the very temple he built, praying ceaselessly for the grace of Sai Baba that may come down pouring on us all in abundance.

After Mahasamadhi

The physical absence of Narasimha Swamiji did create a vacuum. Initially the attendance at the temple diminished, but over the years it has increased by leaps and bounds.

Narasimha Swamiji was a great lover of books. He had collected over 6,000 books on religion, philosophy etc., The Narasimha Swamiji Memorial Library and Free Reading Room was opened by Sri B.N.Datar, the then Union Minister of State for Home Affairs on the first 'Aradhana' day of Swamiji in October 1957. From 1957 onwards the Annual Aradhana Day is celebrated as Founders Day at the All India Sai Samaj.

Narasimha Swamiji felt 'Bhajan' is the life of Sai movement. Sri Narasimha Swamiji Dwarakamayi Prathama Sishya Ghosti led by Sundareswara Iyer was systematically performing Bhajans on all Saturdays. From 1959 onwards, *dhanurmasa bhajan* in the early morning is also undertaken. Sri Gopalakrishna Bhagavathar started 'Radha Kalyan' in January 1959 and this has become an annual feature. Narasimha Swamiji started *Laksharchanas* to Sai Baba even in the forties and this was upgraded to 'Koti Archana' in 1966.

In 1958, Sri V.S.Ramaswamy Iyengar, a senior Railway official brought fire from the Shirdi 'Dhuni'. This was kept in the 'Homakundam' in front of the shrine and kept alive continuously. Another devotee, Sri N.K.Subba Rau, gifted a Dwarakamayi picture of Sai Baba. He also contributed for construction of a room where *Dhuni* as well as Dwarakamayi picture of Sai Baba are placed.

The picture of Krishna-Rama-Siva-Marutyadi Rupa Sai, which was in the front hall, was shifted to the rear of the Mandir to a small niche under the neem-aswatha tree to serve as 'Gurusthan'. In 1962, an annexe was built to the east of the dispensary to function as the Dental Block.

Narasimha Swamiji's masterpiece is 'Life of Sai Baba' in four volumes. The first two volumes were published before his Mahasamadhi and the other two posthumously. This work of over one thousand pages is a comprehensive biography of Sai Baba dealing with all aspects and is indeed a unique treasure for all Sai devotees. It has already gone into several reprints.

Narasimha Swamiji's cottage is just behind the temple. All the articles sanctified by the touch of Swamiji are preserved there. A marble idol of Narasimha Swamiji has been installed there. Devotees visiting his shrine feel his living presence there.

During Swamiji's time, the main hall of the temple was zinc sheet roofed and in its place, a pucca RCC roofed hall with inverted beams was constructed and this new hall was inaugurated by Justice Sri M.B. Rege on 'Guru Poornima' day in July 1966. On this occasion, the fourth volume of 'Life of Sai Baba' was also released along 'Charters and Sayings' in Tamil, Telugu, Kannada, Gujrathi and Malayalam.

The thatched roofed structure temporarily put up to carry on Sai Baba's pooja during the construction of the main hall was converted into a pucca building and a beautiful life size portrait of Radha Krishna brought from Brindavan was installed there.

As a result of Narasimha Swamiji's work princely revenue was received by the Shirdi Samsthan from pilgrims from various parts of the country. The Shirdi Samsthan nominated Narasimha Swamiji as a member of the Executive committee of the Samsthan. Due to his physical inability Narasimha Swamiji, declined this offer and on his behalf deputed Sri Radhakrishna Swamiji and after 1952 Sri P.Gopalaswamy Iyer to represent him on the Executive Committee of Shirdi Samsthan.

In 1964, the All India Sai Samaj had to face litigation on the subject of the temple being brought under the control of the Hindu Religious Endowment Act by the Government of Tamil Nadu. However, due to Swamiji's grace the High Court of Madras gave a landmark judgment that the All India Sai Samaj did not come under the Hindu Religious Endowment Act.

On 26th January 1966, Narasimha Swamiji's portrait was placed at the feet of Sai Baba in Shirdi and later displayed in the hall along with pictures of intimate devotees of Sai Baba. Sri Sagun Meru Naik, a contemporary devotee of Sai Baba, had great regards for Narasimha Swamiji and as desired by him, Swamiji's portrait was taken in procession along all the streets of Shirdi before being placed at the holy feet of Sai Baba by Justice Sri M.B.Rege. He declared that as long as Sai Baba's name is there, the name of Narasimha Swamiji would also remain linked to that. What a prophetic declaration about a great apostle by a great devotee of a great Master!

In January 1980, Sri Radhakrishna Swamiji attained Mahasamadhi and his portrait has been installed in the Samadhi Mandir Hall at Shirdi.

In 1967, as per the wishes of Sri Godavari Mathaji, a portrait of Narasimha Swamiji was displayed at Upasini Baba's ashram at Sakori. Ramana Ashram at Tiruvannamalai also has displayed since 2001, a portrait of Narasimha Swamiji due to an initiative by Swamiji's devotees at Bangalore.

Swamiji was for 'Vidya dhan'. In July 1967, Justice Sri M.B.Rege inaugurated Sai Vidyalaya. It started functioning with kindergarten classes and first two standards. Over the years it has further developed into a leading school.

1968 was a memorable year for the All India Sai Samaj. It was 50th year of Sai Baba's 'Mahasamadhi'. A 'Bhagavatha Mela' was organised and Sri Gopalakrishna Bhagavatar presided over. A soul-stirring 'Rasa Lila' programme was conducted for nine days and thus attracted thousands of devotees. On Baba's Mahasamadhi 'Swarnapushpa archana' was performed with 108 gold lockets.

The Samaj premises looked like a veritable paradise and Justice Sri M.B.Rege exclaimed – "Who says Baba is only at Shirdi? See the glory of the Master here!"

In 1971, the main hall was decorated all around with colourful pictures portraying the life and *lilas* of Sai Baba. This was followed by the construction of a kitchen for preparation of 'prasad' and a dining hall. At this time, Narasimha Swamiji's cottage was converted into a 'Dhyana Mantap'.

In 1974, the All India Sai Samaj and the *Upasamajams* celebrated the birth centenary of Narasimha Swamiji on a grand scale all over the country. A Sai Devotees' Convention was also held at that time.

In February 1987, a marble idol of Sai Baba was installed at the All India Sai Samaj. 'Kumbhabhishekam' was also performed at that time.

In June 1991, the Golden Jubilee of the All India Sai Samaj was celebrated. To commemorate the Golden Jubilee, ENT and Eye blocks were annexed to the Sai Dispensary. Another highlight of this jubilee was a gathering of contributors to various Sai magazines.

During 1998-2000 various books of Narasimha Swamiji, which were out of print, were reprinted.

In June 2002, the Diamond Jubilee of the All India Sai Samaj was celebrated on a grand scale. A Sai Devotees' convention was held at that time. A special feature was bringing out all the four volumes of 'Life of Sai Baba' as a single attractive book. This popular measure was an instant success and the copies were sold out very fast thus a second edition became necessary.

We have described so far as to what happened at the headquarters of the All India Sai Samaj. Narasimha Swamiji had an all India stature and he is revered all over the country. A few instances are cited here. Sri D.Durgaiah Naidu, a Permanent Way Inspector of the B.N.Railway at Waltair derived inspiration from reading Narasimha Swamiji's books on Sai Baba. He was cured of his long standing bowel complaints by praying to Sai Baba. He raised a sizable amount by public subscriptions and succeeded by Sai Baba's grace in building a cottage in Shirdi for the benefit of the pilgrims coming from South India. The Shirdi Samsthan now uses this house as a hospital. Every brick of this building reverberates with the contribution of Narasimha Swamiji to the Sai movement and Swamiji's impact on Sri Durgaiah Naidu.

A marble idol of Narasimha Swamiji was installed in the sanctum sanctorum of Sri Sai Spiritual Centre, Thyagarajanagar, Bangalore in January 1993. In August 2004 at Vasanthapura (Bangalore) Temple also, Swamiji's marble idol was installed. At the Sai Temple at Malleswaram, Bangalore, worship of Narasimha Swamiji is being done through a life size portrait. At Nava Mithra Mandali, Mumbai, devotees celebrate enthusiastically Narasimha Swamiji's Jayanthi, and Aradhana regularly. At all the *Upasamajams* affiliated to the All India Sai Samaj, devotees worship Narasimha Swamiji. These are only a few examples as every Sai devotee is eternally thankful to Narasimha Swamiji for guiding him to Sai Marg.

Even fifty years after he attained Mahasamadhi, Narasimha Swamiji is always with us in his subtle form. He is blessing us forever. There is no death for a great saint like Narasimha Swamiji. It is our sincere prayer to Samartha Sadguru Sainatha Maharaj, Sadguru Sri Narasimha Swamiji and Sadguru Sri Radhakrishna Swamiji to shower their benign grace on one and all. By their grace, let the Sai movement gain the greatest momentum! Let Sai devotees get the required impetus, inspiration and strength to serve as beacon to humanity and reach loftier heights in their spiritual pursuits!

Comrades in Baba's service

Dedicated workers, who toil shoulder to shoulder under the inspiration and leadership of Narasimha Swamiji, the founder President of the All India Sai Samaj, contribute their share to the success and growth of a movement in the same way as the originator. As we cannot think of Narasimha Swamiji without thinking of Sai Baba, so we cannot remember him separately from those who worked with him when he launched the movement. It is these comrades in Baba's service who have kept the movement active and shape out its progress after the Mahasamadhi of Narasimha Swamiji.

Sai Baba's grace and Narasimha Swamiji's dynamism drew numerous devotees. In the early years of its publication, 'Sai Sudha' carried in its pages several statements of experiences of devotees, articles and songs and poems in English, Tamil and Telugu from grateful devotees on Sai Baba, his miracles and glory. These writers may all be valued as workers in the cause. The songs by S.Rajam, Lalitha and Suddhananda Bharati Swamiji proved very popular and they are sung in bhajans in Sai Temples. The Dwarakamayi Bhajana Ghosti in Madras led by Sri Sundaresha Iyer, has rendered yeoman service in this regard.

At the All India Sai Samaj, Madras, Messrs. P.Panini Rao, A. Varadappa Chettiyar, P.Gopalaswamy, Abdul Karim Sahib (Forest Officer), W.V.Rajan, C.V.Rajan, A.M.Sivaraman and others stood by Narasimha Swamiji by serving as Vice Presidents and committee members.

Among the Secretaries, Messrs. O.K.Varada Rao, M.D.Krishna Murthy and V.K.Panthulu, T.Keshava Rao, S.Seshadri call for special mention.

In the districts Messrs. B.R.Ranganathan of Poona, T.G.K.Murthy of Srirangam, K.Sadagopan of Pondicherry, T.L.S.Mani Iyer of Kumbhakonam, D.Raghunatha Rao of Omalur and Dr.M.K.Rajagopalachari of Nellore and others too numerous to mention here, have derived inspiration and have carried out good work in their particular areas.

Sri Radhakrishna Swamiji evolved himself to be the disciple and spiritual heir to Sri Narasimha Swamiji. He was deputed in 1952 to Bangalore to spread Sai Baba's message in Bangalore and Karnataka.

Swami Keshavaiah who was a Sub Registrar in Andhra Pradesh distinguished himself for performing Sai worship with single minded devotion.

Basheer Baba of Kadapah in Andhra Pradesh took up Sai propagation inspired by Narasimha Swamiji. He attained several 'siddhis' due to the benevolence of Sai Baba. He took the torch of the Sai movement to Srilanka, Burma, Thailand, Japan, Egypt. Lagos and other Middle East countries. He organised the World Sai Prachar Sabha.

Rao Sahib B.Papaiah Chetty of Nellore was inspired by Narasimha Swamiji's book 'The Charters and Sayings'. Sai Baba instructed him to donate a princely sum of Rs.11,455/- to Narasimha Swamiji in 1940. This became the nucleus for starting the All India Sai Samaj at Madras.

Sri D.Bhima Rao who was the Post Master General of Madras succeeded Narasimha Swamiji as President of the All India Sai Samaj and held this position upto 1970.

Sri A.V.K.Chari of Coimbatore was a political leader till he met Narasimha Swamiji in 1941. He assisted Swamiji actively and was responsible for laying a firm foundation for Sai mission in the Coimbatore area.

Sri K.R.S.Iyer, a distant relative of Narasimha Swamiji in his 'poorvashram' life, was influenced by him to take up Sai worship and he was totally involved in Sai Samaj activities after his retirement from service.

Arthur Osborne, a native of Australia was influenced by Narasimha Swamiji to take up Sai worship. His book 'The Incredible Sai Baba' has reached readers overseas. Narasimha Swamiji took Sai Baba out of Maharashtra and made him known all over India. Arthur Osborne took Sai Baba from Narasimha Swamiji's writings and placed him as a world figure.

Sri J.N.Bose of Kolkata met Narasimha Swamiji in 1940 or so and by the *udhi* given by him, his son recovered from an illness. He assisted Narasimha Swamiji in carrying out Sai propagation in Bengal and Assam. He has translated several books of Swamiji into Bengali.

Smt.Mani Sahukar, a social worker in Mumbai, was influenced by Narasimha Swamiji to take up Sai Baba's worship in unusual circumstances in 1943. She has written a book 'Sai Baba – the Saint of Shirdi' with a foreword from Narasimha Swamiji. This book is quite popular in our country as well as overseas. She has delivered lectures on Sai Baba at many forums in India and abroad and has contributed to Sai movement considerably.

Sri A.Varadappa Chettiyar, a social worker and Presidency Magistrate was closely associated with Narasimha Swamiji for twenty years, assisting him in Sai prachar. Sri J.D.Pannalal, a Presidency Magistrate actively assisted Narasimha Swamiji in the building projects of the All India Sai Samaj. He was Treasurer of the All India Sai Samaj for a long time.

Epilogue

———◆———

This book *Sri Narasimha Swami: Apostle of Shirdi Sai Baba* – containing the unique story of Narasimha Swamiji is quite fascinating. It is indeed a sacred story to read and recapitulate. Narasimha Swamiji himself has written his story and I am only an instrument. Leaving aside great scholars and men of wisdom, Narasimha Swamiji has chosen me as his instrument. I am only a common man without any learning or knowledge of scriptures. Is this not a great wonder?

Narasimha Swamiji's story will remove the three fold afflictions. Even a cursory reading of his life story would enable one to get abundant spiritual benefit. Therefore please read this book lovingly so that crores of your sins will be destroyed. Those who want to escape the cycle of births and deaths, should follow Narasimha Swamiji's advice to cultivate a ceaseless devotion to the holy feet of Sai Baba and to chant his holy name 'Sai Ram'. Once the mind is completely filled with 'Sai', that is renunciation of worldly life!

I bow down to Narasimha Swamiji, to whom all devotees are equal, who knows no respect or disrespect, whose mind has no likes and dislikes and who shows not the slightest inequality in his treatment of others.

May this sacred book find a place in the homes of all, for daily reading. For it will ward off all the difficulties of the reader. When the book is read with reverence, Sai Samarth is pleased and destroys the poverty of ignorance, giving the reader wealth and prosperity of knowledge.

It was Sai Baba's plan to bring out this work. Blessed is the life of that devotee who is firmly attached to His feet. He who has any thought for his own good should read Narasimha Swamiji's story sincerely. And birth after birth, he will happily remember Sai's beneficence.

Oh readers, let me pray to Narasimha Swamiji. Oh Gurudeva, burn down my karma and *akarma* (inaction), ward off my bad qualities, and dispel delusions born of 'maya'. Clear my mind of doubts and make me steadfast and firm of purpose. I do not want merit nor do I want sin. In truth, relieve me from the cycle of births and deaths.

Oh Gurudeva, when I surrender at your feet, you stand on all my four sides. Your presence fills all the places and you dwell in me too! Or rather, the idea of separateness between 'you' and 'me' is painful indeed. Hence I surrender to you to attain upliftment.

Oh Gurudeva, *Sri Narasimha Swami: Apostle of Shirdi Sai Baba* – while making this biography, you have brought forth a miracle indeed. You have written your story, for the upliftment of your devotees.

I am only a namesake. It is impossible to write your story for a lowly creature like me. I do not have the capacity to chronicle the life of a saint of your eminence. I have only a doubting unbelieving mind. Never have I done 'Upasana' with a steadfast mind nor have I sung 'bhajans' with all intensity. And it was with such hands that you have got your life story written, to show to the world, that you are the author. Can a fly ever lift the Meru mountain? Or a lapwing suck the ocean? But when the Sadguru stands behind you, he makes marvelous things happen!

And so, my Guru bandhus, I now make obeisance to you. This book is complete and is offered at his feet. Such a book, when studied will satisfy one's desires. When Sadguru's feet are clasped to the heart, the ocean of worldly life will be crossed over safely. Those affected with disease will regain health; the poor will become wealthy, doubts and misconceptions will give way to stability and peace and even the poor and the abject will become generous. By reading this book repeatedly, those suffering from demonic possession or fits of Epilepsy will become free of them.

Even the dumb, disabled, the lame and the deaf, by reading this will be happy. Even those who are engulfed by ignorance, will be uplifted.

Incomprehensible are the doings of Narasimha Swamiji. He has firmly and totally absorbed me at his feet and making me serve him, he has got this work completed through me.

In the end, I offer my pen and my mind, without any reservation, at the feet of the Trinity – Sai Baba, Sri Narasimha Swamiji and Sri Radhakrishna Swamiji, who control and sustain the whole world and inspire the mind. May their blessings be on one and all.

Part-V

Some Reminiscences

Concept of surrender

by

Sri Narasimha Swamiji

———◆———

Sai Baba has granted the prayer of my life for an increased and still increasing measure of self-surrender by promoting in me *ananya chinta*. That is intense and unceasing concentration on him (total and exclusive concentration on Sai Baba) based on the realization that he is looking after all my needs and responsibilities, such as they might be, after my passing into *Vanaprastha Ashrama*, thus ensuring me deep mental peace.

In November 1937, I was at Tiruvannamalai and intended to start for Madras by train. A friend, Sri Tulasidas P.Sahani, offered to take me to Madras in his car, wherein he, Smt.Uma and I could sing bhajans or 'Namavalis' all along the 140 miles of the journey. It was raining and I consulted Sai Baba by prayerfully casting a chit at random. Sai Baba's direction was that I should go by train. I went to my friend and apologized for my not being able to join the bhajan party; but he pleaded with me to change my mind.

I returned to my quarters and pleaded with Sai Baba. The rule with Sai Baba was and is that once a decision is given, a second consultation on the same matter should not be sought because "Sai Ramo Dwirnabhibhashate" – Sai Baba does not revise or reverse his decision.

I, however, pleaded with Sai Baba that he should permit me to transgress his orders for that once, as the object of the transgression was pious. And I also prayed, that, for the same reason, the penalty that was bound to follow the transgression be lenient.

Then I started with the two pious friends in Sri Tulasidas's car. It was raining on and off the entire day and all along the way. But we were cheerful, singing bhajans and Namavalis and the journey started very pleasantly.

As a result of the inclement weather, the car was proceeding slowly. After the fifth mile, suddenly we heard the sound of something snapping and the car shuddered to a halt. Sri Tulasidas alighted and found that the rear axle had broken. Thus the journey came to an abrupt end.

It was still raining. There was no kind of shelter nearby at the place where the car had broken down. And, of course, getting the car repaired was out of question. It was then that I revealed to my friends that I had joined them in their journey by car against the express direction of Sai Baba.

I at once submitted myself to Sai Baba, thanked him for the lightness of the penalty and prayed for direction whether I should, at that stage, try to go by train or should continue the journey by car. This was all very good, to make such a request, but how was I to get a car which would take me to Madras?

Sri Tulasidas's car would take at least one full day to be repaired and made fit for journey. But in the meanwhile, what were we to do in the pouring rain on the desolate road?

After I waited for about an hour along with my companions, knowing neither what to do nor what would happen to us, a car coming from Tiruvannamalai drew up alongside. Sri P.Krishnamachari, Salesman of Volkart Brothers, Madras, was at the wheel and the sole occupant of the car. He offered to take me and Smt.Uma in his car.

As soon as we got in, Sri Krishnamachari remarked that events since that morning had been puzzling him. Earlier in the day he had written home to Madras that they need not expect him at Madras for another four days as he had decided to extend his stay at Tiruvannamalai. But at about 11 am something made him suddenly change his mind and he wished to start for Madras.

He could not discern any clear reason for this change of mind. He went to Sri Ramana Maharishi, at whose Ashram he had been staying and asked for permission to leave. The permission was readily granted and he at once started off to Madras and unexpectedly caught up with us, stranded on the road.

Sri Krishnamachari said that his sudden change of decision and the urgency he felt to get back to Madras ceased to be a riddle when he saw our helpless condition and us. It was because we were stranded helplessly that God must have made him change his mind so that he could come to our rescue, he concluded.

I confirmed his belief. I said it was Lord Sainath who had instructed on my behalf. It was he who had asked me to go to Madras by car, at 11 am. It was only he who could find a car to take my companion and me to Madras. And he did it, because he alone could and did change Krishnamachari's mind to serve a higher and benign purpose.

Shubra Marga

(My first meeting with Sri Narasimha Swamiji at Ooty)

by

Sri Radhakrishna Swamiji

———•—•———

I could not resist the urge to place on record Sri Narasimha Swamiji's words to me at the very first meeting I had with him. The hope that Narasimha Swamiji's words will provide guidance to Sai Bhaktas and seekers of truth, have helped me to overcome the great diffidence I felt in making public this intensely personal experience.

Narasimha Swamiji's advice only shows how Sai Baba's loving kindness was showered on me through his great apostle, revered Narasimha Swamiji.

After this there have been many such experiences, which have helped me in my evolution in the spiritual path. Sai Baba has paved the way for me for a worthy living to realize Truth. Sai Baba is all in one to me – mother, father, relative, friend, knowledge, wealth and all.

What more can I say? He gave us plenty of opportunities to realize *Samatva*, enough power to bear 'sukha' and 'dukha' (pleasure and pain) and so on, equally, without hurting myself. Enough patience he has showered on this humble self on this path of spirituality.

Sri Narasimha Swamiji had said: - "The Supreme Light Divine shines in every heart. Thus everyone is immortal. You need not search for it. Simply ask for it and it shall be given to you.

1. "Remember Baba has form and he is formless too. Do not begin to analyse the quality of the metal but drink the milk from the container.

2. "Stick to the spirit. Sainath leads you into the kingdom of spirit. He has vouchsafed to those who approach him the white path, the *Shubra Marga*. Do not doubt it. He will pour the essence in you after removing the age-long dirt in you.

3. "Remember his words – *Ughe muge* – sit quiet. Have patience and at the end you will have the reward. Concentrate on his feet first and then go on upwards. You will get the grace in full with all *ananda*.

4. "There is no difference between Brahma, Vishnu, Maheswara and Sai Baba. The three combined in one you will be able to find in Sai Baba, too, the pure unadulterated omnipotent Soul. He lavishes his grace freely upon all devotees that take shelter at his feet.

5. "Sincerely approach him straight. Breathe your full life in him, and your eternal rest. Are you prepared? If so, start from this very moment itself.

6. "Go and enter straight into your heart and live with him. He is your mother. He knows your hunger and will feed you at all times.

7. "Take the banner of Sai Baba's love and compassion and propagate for the rest of your life. This is your Guru Seva. Mere learning and living with all comforts in life is not worth anything at all. May Sai Baba's grace be with you forever. Be happy and live with courage. Sai Baba will take care of you. Don't fear. Walk on the spiritual path courageously and I am with you.

8. "Remember my case, how I have been divested of all my belongings, before he took possession of me,"

Some Reminiscences

In the course of his long and eventful life, both as a lawyer and politician and later as the itinerant evangelist of the Sai movement, Narasimha Swamiji travelled all over India and many people came into contact with him.

Following are a few reminiscences. (Some of them have been culled from the speeches and writings of the persons concerned).

Justice Sri M.B.Rege, High Court Judge, Indore:

Sri Narasimha Swamiji is a personality by himself and, spiritually as well, his disciplined behaviour and punctuality are praise-worthy and are worthy of emulation. He possesses a heart of gold and his services to humanity through 'Guru Seva' is politically, religiously and spiritually commendable.

Narasimha Swamiji's sacrifice is greater than the sacrifice of any of us in the service of Sai Baba.

We are lucky, indeed, that we have the physical Sai Baba in the form of Sri Narasimha Swamiji along with Sai Baba's spirit – a remarkable case of two in one.

Swami Sivananda, Divine Life Society, Rishikesh:

Sri Narasimha Swamiji is really a blessed and saintly soul. He also had the intense *sowbagya* fortune of being mysteriously drawn to Sainath Maharaj who had lovingly revealed to him the divine swaroopa. The joy of his discovery and revelation has fired

Narasimha Swamiji with an intense desire to share his blessedness with one and all in this sacred land.

I was one of the lucky recipients of Narasimha Swamiji's goodwill and affection. He assigned me the editorship of the moral and spiritual teachings bequeathed to us by Sai Baba and the magazine published from All India Sai Samaj -'Sai Sudha'.

Kaviyogi Swami Suddhananda Bharati:
What is impossible for faith? What is rare for a strong devoted soul? What saint Paul, Ananda, St.Francis, Swami Vivekananda achieved for their teachers, Sri Narasimha Swamiji has achieved for his impersonal Master, the wonderful Sai Baba.

Swami Rajeswarananda:
Man needs today not more drugs but health; not more of laws but honesty; not more law but more love; not more knowledge but culture and character; not more societies but unity; not more nations but humanity; and not more doctrines and dogmas but divinity. Our Narasimha Swamiji stands for such a life.

Narasimha Swamiji and myself were staying together at Ramanashram for sometime and drinking deep the nectar of bliss.

Sri C.Rajagopalachari (in a speech at Salem):
Sri Narasimha Swamiji and myself are childhood friends. When we grew up both of us took up the legal profession. Strangely enough when we bade goodbye to Salem, each of us left Salem in response to a different set of circumstances and each took a different path. While I went to what might be called the political 'Ashram' at Tiruchengode, Narasimha Swamiji went to the spiritual ashram of Ramana at Tiruvannamalai.

Sri B.N.Datar, Hon'ble Minister of State for Home Affairs, Government of India, New Delhi
Sri Narasimha Swamiji's life has been an inspiration to all who cared to know the exact meaning of life.

Many of us know how to accumulate wealth, but very few of us know how to renounce wealth. Therefore, I value more not only the renunciation of worldly life virtually, but also the great service that he rendered in the cause of religion and spirituality.

Just as Mahatma Gandhi created mass consciousness about freedom among the Indian people, Narasimha Swamiji created throughout the length and breadth of our country the taste for Sai devotion.

Thanks to Narasimha Swamiji all this has happened, and Sai Baba's name has become a household word everywhere in India. It has captured the hearts of every one of us everywhere. Narasimha Swamiji has changed the face of India as far as Sai devotion is concerned.

Sri V.M.Ramaswami Iyer:

I have known Sri Narasimha Swamiji from his student days. Even in his youth, Narasimha Swamiji had a religious bent of mind. At school he was attracted by the life of Jesus Christ and studied the Bible.

Later he was attracted by the life of Sri Sorakkai Swamiji who had his ashram near Vellore and, at his expense Narasimha Swamiji wrote a biography of this Swamiar and distributed it free.

No doubt, because of his able advocacy and eloquence, Narasimha Swamiji established himself as a leader of the legal profession in Salem; what, however, won him the love and life-long attachment of his clients was his kindliness and compassion for the suffering clients.

Sri J.N.Bose, Kolkata:

It was in 1941 that I had the rare luck of meeting Sri Narasimha Swamiji in Kolkata. He taught me many valuable teachings of Sai Baba.

The remarkable thing about Sri Narasimha Swamiji was that in features and appearance he resembled the Rishis of the Vedic age. He never wasted even a minute's time excepting for a short sleep at night. He used to write something on Sai Baba or talk about him whenever a devotee came to him. Even during his train journeys, he used to write books.

Sri S.Ramanathan

I met Narasimha Swamiji just a few hours before he passed away on 19th October 1956 and I was amazed to see that Swamiji was totally unconcerned and fearless about death. The usual peace and calmness of his mind radiated on his face. Trusting God and his Guru, Swamiji had conquered death. Though he is no more physically, he will guide the destiny of the Sai movement in our country.

Prof.K.R.R.Sastri:

I met the veteran lawyer-politician Narasimha Iyer in Salem in 1920 when I was the Presiding Officer at a polling booth. In 1941 I met him at Madras after his renunciation. Later I met him in Allahabad when he addressed five public meetings on Sai Baba.

Assiduous students would find that both Ramana and Sai Baba attracted not merely Hindus but Muslims and others. Both upheld the equal validity of all religions. Sai Baba, after treading both the Muslim and Hindu paths, guided all. Ramana Maharishi had devotees from all faiths. It is a striking coincidence that the world outside knew of both these saints through the pioneering studies of Narasimha Swamiji.

Prof.K.Panchapagesan, Pudukkottai

Not content with the blessings of personal 'moksha' and salvation, Sri Narasimha Swamiji had, with characteristic generosity of purpose, faith and flaming devotion to the message of the Lord, awakened other slumbering souls and baptized them into a new life and a new sense of realization of the eternal spiritual values.

Sri P.Panini Rao, President, All India Sai Samaj

Narasimha Swamiji was a simple soul with the heart of a child. While exhorting the people to surrender themselves to the will of

Sai Baba and place before him their troubles, Narasimha Swamiji used to ask the devotees who needed guidance in choosing a course of action to write out the several options to their problems on bits of papers, fold them up, put them up before Sai Baba's picture, and pick up one of the bits. This was a way of making a choice with divine guidance by drawing lots.

Sri K.P.Ramakrishna Iyer, Advocate, Madras:

Sri Narasimha Swamiji was instrumental in spreading the gospel of Sai Baba among the people. There was a personal magnetism in him, as was evidenced by the fact that many were inspired to come under Sai Baba's influence and immensely benefited by his mission and teachings

Seek the Light within!
(Sri Narasimha Swamiji's message to readers)

———•+•———

One should raise oneself by the Self; for the Self (*Atman*) alone is the friend of oneself, and the egoistic (lower) self alone is the real enemy of oneself, He is the real light in the form of consciousness 'Sat-Chit-Ananda' abiding in all beings, and all beings abide in the self: Paramatman.

He is the Light of lights who dispels the ignorance of the true seeker. He who, having realized the true nature of the self, perceives everything equally in all beings and everywhere, is regarded as the highest.

He is the true light within you. Call him 'God' or the 'Supreme Being', the one without a second, of Consciousness-Absolute or Paramatman or whatever you like. He is the 'Sat-Chit-Ananda', Bliss Absolute. Meditate on Him. He is the one Reality. Om

Guru's Grace

———◆———

"Everything needs Guru's grace. When Guru's grace descends, the heart blossoms forth like a lotus when the sun shines upon it. When thus opened, he feels that his heart encompasses the whole world of his relationships and shapes his conduct and destiny through the promptings of his heart.

A kind heart is a spring of joy to all within its reach. So let everyone allow his or her heart to speak and tread in the paths of spiritual life refreshing the shade of Truth and Love.

I feel forlorn in Sai-Love. He has possessed me and I have surrendered my all to that 'Living Chaitanya.'

- Sri Narasimha Swamiji

A Brief Profile of Author

Dr G. R. Vijayakumar hails from the Karnataka and settled down in Bangalore. He needs no introduction to Sai-devotees as over 1,500 of his articles have been published in several Sai magazines and souvenirs in the last three decades.

An MBBS, MD from Bangalore university, Dr. Vijayakumar served as an Industrial Physician for 35 years and retired as Chief Medical Officer of Ashok Leyland, an automobile manufacturing industry in Tamil Nadu. Currently he is engaged as a professor Emeritus in Public Health at Rajiv Gandhi University of Health Science in Karnataka and also as a consultant in an AIDS prevention project.

He received the Tamil Nadu state government award in 2009 for donating his blood 103 times. The USAID (United States Agency for International Development) honoured him in 2006 for his pioneering work in AIDS prevention.

www.ingramcontent.com/pod-product-compliance
Lightning Source LLC
Chambersburg PA
CBHW060325050426

42449CB00011B/2648